PATHS
OF
PURE VISION

The Histories, Views, and Practices
of Tibet's Living Spiritual Traditions

BY SHAR KHENTRUL JAMPHEL LODRÖ

TRANSLATED BY MICHAEL R. SHEEHY

Dzokden

Author: Shar Khentrul Jamphel Lodrö
Translator: Michael R. Sheehy

First Edition

ISBN (Paperback): 978-1-958229-04-0
ISBN (ePub): 978-1-958229-05-7

Published by:
DZOKDEN

This work was produced by Dzokden, a not-for-profit organization run entirely by volunteers. This organization is devoted to propagating a non-sectarian view of all the world's spiritual traditions and teaching Buddhism in a way that is completely authentic, yet also practical and accessible to Western culture. It is especially dedicated to propagating the Jonang tradition, a rare jewel from remote Tibet which holds the precious Kalachakra teachings.

For more information on scheduled activities or available materials, or if you wish to make a donation to support our work, please contact:

DZOKDEN
3436 Divisadero Street
San Francisco, California
USA 94123

www.dzokden.org

For each ailment there is a medicine.
If a path is not suitable for one,
it will definitely be suitable for another.
This is the essence of the Rimé Philosophy.

— *Khentrul Rinpoché* —

TABLE OF CONTENTS

THE DALAI LAMA

༄༅། །འཛམ་གླིང་མཁན་པོ་འཛམ་དཔལ་རྫོ་རྗེ་གྲོས་ནས་བོད་གངས་ཅན་སྙིངས་
སུ་དར་བའི་ཆོ་ནན་ས་དགེ་བཀའ་རྙིང་པོན་དང་བཅས་པའི་ཆོས་བརྒྱུད་ཀྱི་ལྟ་གྲུབ་
ལོ་རྒྱུས་རོབ་བརྗོད་ཞིག་ཕྱིས་འདུག་པ། རྗོ་གསར་ཆོས་བརྒྱུད་ཁག་གི་གནས་ཚུལ་
དོན་གཉེར་ཅན་ལ་ཕན་ཐོགས་ཡོང་ངེས་སུ་མཐོང་། རང་རེ་གངས་ལྗོངས་ཀྱི་སྲིས་
མཆོག་ལྷ་མ་གོང་མ་རྣམས་ཀྱི་ལྟ་གྲུབ་བཞིན་སྲོལ་ལཁག་གདུལ་བྱའི་ཁམས་དང་མོས་
པ་དང་དམ་པ་རང་རང་གི་ཉམས་སྲོང་བཅས་དང་བསྟུན་ནས་གསུང་སྲངས་མི་འདྲ་
བ་དང་། དམ་པ་ཕན་ཚུན་ལྱུང་རིགས་ཀྱིས་དགག་གཞན་མཛད་པའི་དག་རྣམ་
དཔྱོད་རྫོ་ཆལ་གོང་དུ་སྙེལ་བའི་ཆེད་དུ་ཡིན་གཤིས། མཐར་ཕྱག་གི་དགོངས་པ་
རྗེ་ཡིན་དཔོག་དཀའ་བས། རང་རང་རྣམ་དཔྱོད་ཤེས་རབ་ཀྱིས་དཔྱད་དེ་བགོ་
སྐལ་ལེན་པར་རིགས། དུས་ཀུན་དགེ་བའི་སྐྱབས་སྣོན་བཅས། ཤཀྱའི་དགེ་སྦྱོང་
དུ་ལའི་བླ་མས། རབ་བྱུང་བཅུ་བདུན་པའི་ཆུ་ལུག་ཟླ་ ༤ ཚེས་ ༡༩ ཕྱི་ལོ་
༢༠༠༣ ཟླ་ ༤ ཚེས་ ༢༡ ལ།།

FOREWORD

By His Holiness the Dalai Lama

In *Paths of Pure Vision*, Khentrul Jamphal Lodro Rinpoche from Dza-mthang Monastery has concisely written on the different lineage accounts, views, and practices of the Jonang, Sakya, Gelug, Kagyu, Nyingma, and Bon spiritual traditions that flourished in the snowy land of Tibet. His hard work has led to presenting these spiritual traditions in ways that bring us fresh understandings and insights into what is most valuable about these traditions.

Our previous sublime teachers and spiritual masters of the Land of Snow taught various views, practices, and customs in different ways, according to personal experiences, dispositions, inclinations, and the varying intellectual capacities of students. Because these authors deliberately developed discernment and sharpness of mind through establishing their refutations based upon Buddhist scriptures and logical reasoning, they were able to be of supreme benefit to beings.

Since the ultimate intent of the Buddha's teachings is difficult to fathom, I urge you to use your own discerning wisdom in order to investigate these teachings, and then determine if they can be accepted and put to good use.

I pray to always be connected to that which is a refuge of virtue.

Shakyamuni Buddha's monk, the Dalai Lama
The sixth month of the Water Sheep year of the Seventeenth Rabjung
August 2003

TRANSLATOR'S PREFACE

Until recently, the Jonang tradition was thought by the world outside of Tibet to be extinct. In the late 1980's, rumors suggested that this Buddhist lineage had survived its seventeenth century persecution in Central Tibet, and in the early to mid 1990's, Western scholars began to make contact with this little known tradition in its homeland of Amdo, Far Eastern Tibet. Today, more than a decade later, we have exemplars of the Jonang such as Khentrul Jamphal Lodro Rinpoche living in the West, giving teachings, transmissions, empowerments, and writing books such as this one.

As the first book in English to situate the Jonang tradition within the context of the four other Tibetan Buddhist traditions and the ancient Bon tradition, *Paths of Pure Vision* is a concise account of the histories, views, and practices of Tibet's major living spiritual traditions. Written over a century after the great luminaries Jamgon Kongtrul Lodro Thaye (1813-1899) and Jamyang Khyentse Wangpo (1820-1892) initiated the Rimed or nonsectarian approach to Tibetan Buddhist philosophy and practice in Eastern Tibet, Khentrul Rinpoche's writings reflect this nonbiased spirit, as well as the Jonang *zhentong* view and Kalachakra lineage that played such an integral dimension in this intellectual movement. As one of the few modern Jonang authors, and a master of the nonsectarian approach, Khentrul Jamphal Lodro Rinpoche offers us insights into both his own Jonang tradition as well as the Rimed vision.

Fortunately, Dr. Cynthia Williams witnessed Khentrul Rinpoche writing *Paths of Pure Vision* on loose sheets of paper with a pencil, as he sat on the floor in a house in Dharamsala, India. With the support of the American Ani Saldron, the Tibetan scholar Tenchong, and the Jonang Tulku Kunga Zangpo, the Tibetan edition of this book was published in New Delhi (Indraprastha Press, 2003). Dr. Williams later asked me to translate this Tibetan book into English. We are now happy to present Khentrul Jamphal Lodro Rinpoche's words and wisdom to the English reading audience.

TECHNICAL NOTES

Due to the rush for publication, the current edition of this book is published Tibetan style, that is, without citations for the quotations embedded within the text. If a future edition is made possible, it is my wish that the references for each of the quotes be cited within the endnotes, and that a complete bibliography of Tibetan sources be made available. An index of names, places, and terms would also be a helpful addition. In this current edition, Tibetan names of texts quoted and numerical listings are provided in Wylie transliteration as annotations within the endnotes. Selected technical Buddhist terms along with their definitions and transliterations are included within the glossary. Names of Tibetan texts are translated into English within the body of the book. Well-known Indian Buddhist philosophical terms such as "Madhyamaka" and "nirvana," as well as Indian names such as "Nagarjuna" are phonetically represented in Sanskrit without diacritics. Keeping true to the Tibetan text, most proper names such as "Dolpopa," places such as "Samye," and popular terms such as "Dzogchen" and "zhentong" are phonetically represented in Tibetan.

ACKNOWLEDGEMENTS

For their support during the process of translating this book, I would like to thank my teacher Khenpo Kunga Sherab Saljay Rinpoche for helping me understand passages on the Six Yogas in this book, and for his guidance in my studies, practice, and translation work; Khentrul Jamphal Lodro Rinpoche for working with me on this translation, and for his patience with my busy graduate student lifestyle; Tulku Kunga Zangpo for his discussions about the Jonang and *zhentong*; Dr. Cynthia A. Williams for her financial support in making this book possible, and for her illimitable enthusiasm for the Jonang; Professor Steven D. Goodman for his continual advisement, and for his suggestions with some of the translation choices; Erik Pema Kunsang, Richard Barron (Chokyi Nyima), Gene Smith, and Cyrus Stearns for their mentorship.

May the Buddhas of the three times smile upon this translation! Sarva Mangalam!

Michael R. Sheehy
Jonang Jamdha Monastery
Buddhist Studies College of Five Sciences
Golok, Amdo, Tibet / Qinghai Province, China
October 21st, 2005

INTRODUCTION
Tibet's Living Traditions

I have written *Paths of Pure Vision* because I have noticed that people from around the world are now taking an interest in Tibetan Buddhism. For instance, Christians and people of different religious faiths, Chinese, Japanese, Burmese, and other Asian Buddhists, scientists without any religious orientations, and in particular, many people from the West have become curious about Tibetan Buddhism. This being the case, I have decided to write this book in order to explain the various traditions of Buddhism in Tibet, and to address some of the complexities regarding these traditions.

Generally speaking, one may wonder if there are differences between the base, path, fruition, and the view, meditation, and conduct of Buddhism from Tibet, and Buddhist traditions from other countries. From a general viewpoint, there are no significant differences in the view, meditation, and conduct of the various Buddhist traditions. Usually discrepancies are perceived due to a lack of experience with the spiritual practices of Buddhism. Although Buddhism has many paths and levels of accomplishment, the Tibetan Buddhist traditions are unique in that they encompass the entirety of what the Buddha taught.

Besides superficial differences in the ways and customs of cultures, the multiple traditions of Buddhism interweave with one another in a single spirit. The reason for this is that all of these teachings come from the same teacher, and all of their teaching techniques are directed towards the same aim of attaining Buddhahood. Nevertheless, although slight differences amongst Buddhist traditions may seem contradictory, their subsidiary practices, how they refine their views, and how they employ their meditation techniques and ethics all reflect the variety of the Buddha's skillful means. Since the Buddha's different teachings are like medicines for curing different kinds of spiritual sicknesses, there is no one teaching or medicine for any particular sickness.

Buddhism is also distinct from other religions in that it offers an extensive science of the mind. This contemplative science has the capacity for detecting through experiential deduction certain unobvious phenomena that modern empirical science is currently incapable of detecting. Because of this, Buddhist meditation practices can be used as a model for modern science in order to study the innermost facets of consciousness. In addition to this, Buddhism contributes a diverse repertoire of ways and means for developing one's interior psychological qualities which is something that modern science is unable to do.

When someone knows how to practice Buddhism unerringly, the ordinary situations of this life are enriched with well-being and happiness. This follows naturally without effort, like wood burning on fire. A Buddhist practitioner discovers how fleeting worldly concerns are not what are most important but what is most important is the continual great bliss that suffuses oneself through successive lifetimes. Being a living spiritual tradition, Buddhism has the incredible capacity to bring about not only temporary well-being, but ultimate happiness for oneself and all living beings. In order to do this, it is imperative that one bring into one's own experience the entire range of positive qualities by cultivating a path of expedient means. Since Tibetan Buddhism incorporates multiple means for attaining enlightenment, many people have taken a keen interest in the Tibetan Buddhist traditions.

Tibetan Buddhism is vast and profound. It encompasses a diversity of instructions on spiritual practice, and it is this diversity that lends itself to the different traditions of Tibetan Buddhism. I have decided to write about the histories, views, and practices of these traditions not because there have not been previous works, as there are many books on these subjects, but because the majority of these works tend to be either inaccessible to the general reader or were written by scholars who are partial towards their own views.

While people from around the world are now showing an interest in studying and comparing the differences between Tibetan Buddhism, and the Buddhist traditions from other countries, because there isn't a thorough understanding of any one tradition, many misunderstandings arise. This has happened in the past, it is happening now, and it will certainly happen in the future. Thinking that the views and practices of the different Buddhist traditions contradict each other, one may conclude that one view is superior while another is inferior. Along these same lines, individuals who do not understand the essence of religion, and who are unfamiliar with the views and practices of Buddhism may misjudge these traditions. For these reasons, it is important to understand the various Buddhist traditions in order to avoid further misunderstandings.

In Tibet, there are now five major Buddhist traditions. These traditions are divided and categorized according to their philosophical and meditative systems. Among these surviving Tibetan Buddhist traditions, the Jonang tradition presents its own distinctive philosophical views and meditative practices. Since it is not included within the official documents of the Tibetan Government in Exile, this tradition is largely unknown to the world outside of the Tibetan plateau. Consequently, many interested readers and Buddhist practitioners have not had access to this living tradition. Taking into consideration that this tradition may be new to many readers, I have written a more detailed account of its history, views, and practices. If for any reason you are unable to read this book from cover to cover, I suggest that you go directly to Chapter VII, as you may find a surprising new story there.

CHAPTER I

THE BON TRADITION

TIBET'S INDIGENOUS RELIGION

Prior to the arrival of Buddhism, the religion of Tibet was "Bon," and "Bonpo" was the name given to Tibetan people. Nowadays, there are various disagreements amongst scholars of Tibet regarding the authenticity of Bon thought, its practices, origins, and how it relates to Buddhism. Some even suggest that Bon was not an actual religion, implying that at the time of the Tibetan Dharma King Trisong Deutsen, the miraculous manifestation Padmasambhava, and the great scholar-bodhisattva Shantarakshita, the Bon tradition was subjugated to the extent that it disappeared. Though it is true that during the seventh and eighth centuries C.E. the Bon tradition degenerated, this could have been due to a lapse in the social status of their thought and practice, or a lapse in the ethics of their scriptures and reasoning. It is also possible that this was due to political persecution.

Some scholars suggest that there are two Bon traditions: the current day tradition known as Yungdrung Bon, and an earlier tradition. This indigenous Bon tradition existed prior to the teacher Shenrab, and because of this, its views and practices are regarded by these scholars as erroneous. Even though this earlier Bon was vanquished by Padmasambhava, there are few who say that the views and practices of today's Yungdrung Bon tradition are perverted. Still, there are others who insist that the earlier Bon was never a genuine tradition, and that today's Bon mimics Buddhism, making present-day Bon an unreal Bon. Taking all of this into consideration, it could be that the current Bon tradition imitated much of Buddhism; on the other hand, Tibetan Buddhism was largely influenced by many of the practices derived from Bon.

In this way, Bon and Buddhism have been absorbed into each other, and have mutually benefited one another. If we can say anything about this, I think that this is the impartial conclusion.

Today, in Tibet as well as in India, the base, path, fruition as well as the view, meditation, and conduct of the Bon tradition is unquestionably authentic. In fact, I have not witnessed even the slightest degree of difference between Bon and Buddhism. With this in mind, it seems worthwhile for Buddhist practitioners to pay equal respect towards and learn about the Bon tradition. I have also met and seen some extraordinary Bon practitioners who exemplify authentic Bon spirituality, giving reason for everyone to learn about this magnificent spiritual tradition.

In the northern snowy direction, on the ground of this jewel-like Earth,
The magical manifestation of wisdom and means, Shenrab Thubpa,
Descended from the long celestial chord of the Yungdrung gods,
Destined for cool Tibet, you are the splendor of excellence!

CHAPTER II

A CONCISE INTRODUCTION TO BUDDHISM

THE TWO TRUTHS

Though there were precursors to the dissemination of Buddhism in Tibet that occurred as early as the fourth century C.E., the actual flourishing of Buddhism in Tibet was initiated during the seventh century C.E. During the eighth century C.E., the Buddhist sutra and tantra teachings were transmitted into Tibet from India. Out of the four philosophical systems representative of Indian Buddhism, the teachings of Madhyamaka or the Middle Way philosophy spread most widely throughout Tibet.[1] In order to more fully explore this topic, I will present a synopsis of the base, path, and fruition along with the view, meditation, and conduct of Buddhism.

There are two truths which are the basis of all objects of knowledge. These two all-encompassing truths are known as the "conventional truth" and the "ultimate truth."[2] Conventional truth is consciousness of ordinary beings, including the ordinary awareness of seeing, hearing, tasting,

---

1   Four philosophical systems (*grub mtha' bzhi*) derived from Indian Buddhism. These are: 1) Sarvastivadin; 2) Vaibhaisika; 3) Yogacara; 4) Madhyamaka.

2   The two kinds of truth are the conventional truth (*kun rdzob bden pa*) which encompasses the relative apparent level of reality, and the ultimate truth (*don dam bden pa*) which encompasses the absolute level of reality.

smelling, and touching as well as the forms, sounds, smells, tastes, and textures which correspond to these types of consciousness. To the unexamined or unanalyzed mind, the temporary co-emergence of consciousness with an object seems real. Because this false experience is unstable and deceptive, it is the truth of conventional reality.

Ultimate truth is what does not naturally appear to the unexamined or unanalyzed minds of ordinary beings. It is the absolute final meaning discovered through logic and reasoning, the nature of all phenomena that is incomprehensible and imperceptible to ordinary minds. This ultimate nature of reality is only directly recognizable during the first stage of the bodhisattva's path towards awakening.[3] Because this is the truth of factual actuality, it is said to be the truth of ultimate reality.

BASE, PATH, FRUITION

Simultaneously perceiving these two levels of reality directly occurs during the omniscience of Buddhahood. These two truths are the basis upon which goodness and badness, happiness and sadness, and everything that can be known are arranged and established. This is the "base" or the "ground" of these two truths.

Next is the "path" or the way in which the two accumulations are acquired. These two are the accumulation of merit and the accumulation of wisdom. The accumulation of wisdom is a process of familiarizing oneself with and understanding the pure absolute abiding reality, then the nature of everything is known. This is not easily realised or taught. The method of realizing how to spontaneously and effortlessly benefit sentient beings as a Buddha in the future is to meditate on bringing forth the qualities of loving-kindness and compassion now. In order to do this, it is essential to practice various different meditations such as those on generosity, equanimity, patience, and so forth.

---

3   There are generally ten levels or stages (*sa bcu*) that a bodhisattva progresses along towards buddhahood.

Realizing the nature of everything knowable Þ the sublime actuality of phenomena Þ is a process of learning that begins with listening, reflecting, and then conjoining analysis with stabilization meditation. Finally, once all of one's inhibitions are exhausted, and there is recognition of how we are endowed with every enlightened quality, Buddhahood is realised. This is the supreme state that each individual is capable of attaining.

The culmination of the path is known as "fruition," the perfected state of Buddhahood. This is the state that has abandoned both the causes and results of unhappiness, while it has disabled one's own patterns of emotional upset from re-occurring so that one is never separated from unchangeable supreme happiness. To attain Buddhahood is to effortlessly and spontaneously benefit beings without end until samsara is completely emptied.

VIEW, MEDITATION, CONDUCT

In order to become a fully realised Buddha, there are three principles known as view, meditation, and conduct. These three form the basis for the four Indian Buddhist philosophical systems: Vaibhashika, Sautrantika, Cittamatra, and Madhyamaka. These are then further characterized into the ordinary and extraordinary vehicles.[4] Through their means and wisdom, the early Dharma Kings, translators, and scholars in Tibet made it so that the Madhyamaka system of the extraordinary vehicles primarily influenced view while the Vaibhashika system of the ordinary vehicle influenced conduct. Consequently, the Madhyamaka view is predominant among Tibetan Buddhist traditions.

Due to slightly different ways and somewhat different techniques of interpreting the Madhyamaka view, there arose different Buddhist traditions in Tibet. However distinctive these interpretations may be, the basis for all of them is the single view of Madhyamaka. This Madhyamaka view is that the actual nature of phenomena, or the way in which every knowable thing

---

4 The "ordinary vehicle" (*theg pa thun mong*) refers to the Hinayana teachings while the "extraordinary vehicles (*theg pa thun mong ma yin pa*) refers to the Mahayana and Vajrayana.

exists, is not the way things appear to us now. Because of this, we think that we see things such as a table, yet if we were to use our logic and investigate more closely, it would become obvious that what we call a "table" is nothing but a conglomeration of tiny parts. In fact, "table" is simply dependent upon these tiny parts, and if we try to establish a truly existing table, we won't be able to find a "table" anywhere. In the same way, everything that can be known is dependent upon its name and identity. Because things have their own basis of dependence, when we search for something, it is impossible to find anything. This is why it is said that all phenomena lack intrinsic existence.

Nevertheless, without investigating, the meaning of conventional phenomena is imputed. This is to say, to minds that don't analyze what can be known, things seem to be the way they appear. This is due to the inevitable fact that causes have their results. This kind of philosophical thinking is how Madhyamaka dispels the two extreme views of absolutism, thinking that things truly exist, and nihilism, thinking that things do not exist. It is safe to say that this Madhyamaka view is common to all traditions of Tibetan Buddhism.

Then, there is meditation and the two accumulations acquired along the path. What is to be cultivated during the practice of meditation is both the mind of awakening, and the two types of selflessness or insubstantiality.[5] Meditation itself is reliant on two methods of training: 1) shamatha or calm-abiding meditation; and 2) vipashyana or insight meditation. A meditation practitioner first listens, and then studies the various ways that phenomena reside. The middle meditative phase is examining and reflecting upon the different conclusions that are drawn from experience. Finally, it is important to stabilize one's meditation one-pointedly and repeatedly on the object of meditation in order to discover, without being deceived.

For example, first we have to hear about how the self seems substantial, and how the self is neither identical with nor distinct from the five

---

5   The two types of selflessness or insubstantiality (bdag gnyis) are that of an intrinsic self and of phenomena.

mental and physical constituents of a sentient being.[6] Once the practitioner understands that there is no essence to the self, the meaning of this is contemplated over and over again. Once a practitioner has cut-through all misconceptions in the meditative state, and has given rise to complete certainty about the meaning being meditated upon, there is the perfection of meditation.

As for conduct, the general way in which Buddhist practitioners conduct themselves is to not to cause any harm. In addition to this, Tibetan Buddhists are all practitioners of the Mahayana vehicle which means that the basis for their behavior is love and compassion. This means acting in a good natured and noble way. Next is to wholeheartedly give rise to bodhicitta or the mind of awakening in order to benefit other living beings. This is the way in which a Tibetan Buddhist practitioner conducts oneself. This conduct is derived from the Vaibhashika Buddhist tradition, and is the ethical way in which ordained Tibetan monks behave. The Vaibhashikas were one of the four main early Indian Buddhist schools of the shravakas, and their ethical guidelines continue to serve as the basis for Buddhist conduct.[7]

---

6   The five constituents (*phung po lnga*) are: 1) form (*gzugs*); 2) sensations (*tshor ba*); 3) perceptions (*'du shes*); 4) dispositions (*'du byed*); 5) consciousness (*rnam shes*). These five constituents comprise the mental and physical components of an individual person.

7   See glossary for "shravaka."

CHAPTER III

THE LIFE OF THE BUDDHA AND BUDDHISM IN INDIA

SHAKYAMUNI'S LIFE STORY

The Buddha has many names. In Tibetan he is known as "Shakya Thubpa," and in Sanskrit, the ancient language of India, he is known as "Shakyamuni." The Buddha was born over two thousand, five hundred years ago in the Indian town of Lumbini, a present day region of Southern Nepal. In order to provide some background, I will elaborate on some references from Buddhist literature. For instance, in the *Sutra of the Encounter of the Master with His Spiritual Son* it reads,[8]

> *In the past, immeasurable cosmic aeons ago, there was a world-system known as "The Buddhafield with as Many Grains of Sand as the Ganges River." In this Buddhafield, there was a tathagata named "Pinnacle of Power." As a Buddha, he tremendously benefited beings before passing into nirvana. Following his Buddhahood, he continued to teach for inconceivable aeons. From that time onwards, he developed a pure mind that vowed to teach the way towards Buddhahood until samsara was emptied.*

---

8   Tibetan title: *yab sras mjal ba'i mdo.*

Our historical Buddha Shakyamuni actually purified the entirety of his de-filements derived from the two types of obscurations immeasurable eons ago, and actualized complete enlightenment.[9] Because of his wisdom, means, and intense compassion, he appeared during the age of the five degenerations.[10] Fortunately, due to his deep consideration and affection for living beings, Shakyamuni manifested in this world and performed the twelve deeds of a supreme emanation body.[11]

The *Sublime Continuum* also states,[12]

Knowing this world, the Great Compassionate One
Gazed upon this entire superficial destructible universe
And, without wavering from the ultimate dimension of reality,
Generated and manifested through various magical manifestations.

Descending from the joyous Tushita Pureland
He entered into his mother's womb and was born.
Learned and skilled in the arts,
He pleased and played with a retinue of consorts.

Then, he renounced his opulent life for austerities.
Proceeding to Bodhgaya.
He subdued hordes of demons
And, after perfect enlightening,

---

9   The two types of obscuration (*sgrib gnyis*) are cognitive and emotional.

10   The five degenerations are: 1) degeneration of lifespan; 2) degeneration of time period; 3) degeneration of views; 4) degeneration of emotional well-being; 5) degeneration of sentient beings.

11   These twelve deeds are: 1) Descending from Tushita Heaven (*'pho ba*); 2) Entering his mother's womb (*lhum zhugs*); 3) Taking birth (*bltams pa*); 4) Becoming skilled in worldly arts and demonstrating physical prowess (*bzo dang*); 5) Enjoying a retinue of queens (*rol rtse*); 6) Renouncing the world (*nges 'byung*); 7) Practicing austerities and renouncing them (*dka' spyad drug*); 8) Going to the essence of enlightenment (*gshegs*); 9) Defeating the demon Mara (*bdud sde bcom*); 10) Attaining total enlightenment under the Bodhi Tree (*byang chub*); 11) Turning the Wheel of Dharma (*chos 'khor*); 12) Departing for nirvana (*myang 'das*).

12   Tibetan title: *rgyud bla ma*.

He turned the wheel of awakening.
Passing into nirvana,
He vowed to teach as long as
Fields of existence remain impure.

By the time our Buddha Shakyamuni had taken rebirth as Dampa Togpar in the Tushita Pureland, he had already manifested as a bodhisattva in various realms of the world. Once he descended from Tushita, he had completed all of his rebirths.

While residing in the Tushita Pureland with the gods during one of the festivals, the Buddha to be became inspired by the celestial sounds of the goddess musicians. Moved by their music, the power of his previous merit, his own innate capacity, and the blessings of previous Buddhas, the bodhisattva descended into our world. At that moment of inspiration, he removed his crown and placed it on top of his regent Maitreya's head.

Considering that the place was Kapilivastu, the caste was regal, the bloodline was Shakya, his mother Maya was more beautiful than a goddess, and that the time was during the five degenerations, the bodhisattva departed for our world. Riding on a cloudy white elephant with six tusks, he magically entered his mother Maya's womb as she purified herself. While in his mother's womb for ten months, the bodhisattva compassionately guided innumerable disciples onto the paths of the three vehicles, helping to bring them into their spiritual maturity.

As an omen of the Buddha's birth, ninety-four million medicinal herbal plants spontaneously sprouted in the center of the great continents of planet Earth while sandalwood forests bloomed on each of the subcontinents. These as well as many other wondrous signs foreshadowed the birth of the Buddha.

When mother Maya was walking through the Lumbini groves, she grasped the limb of a Palkasha tree with her right hand, stretched out her body, and without any pain, gave birth to the Buddha to be. Upon his arrival, he stepped upon lotus flowers that grew in each of the four directions. Witnessing these and many other miraculous signs, his father named him

Siddhartha, meaning "the one who fulfills every purpose." As a child he was pampered by thirty-two maidens, and because of his carefulness and gentle nature, he was called the "Sage of the Shakya clan" or "Shakyamuni." Among the many fortunetellers and saints that visited him as a child, it was Rishi Nagpo Nyonmong Med who prophesized him to become a Buddha.

As a young man, the bodhisattva went to school in order to mature his various skills. Siddhartha excelled in his studies and in particular, his study of language. His understanding of languages was so great that he knew languages that his teacher Kungi Shenyen had never even heard of. At the age of sixteen, he defeated the strongest of the young dexterous Shakya warriors in competitive sporting events, and he later married the princess Drag Zinma. Along with his wife, and lover Ri Dwags Kayma, Siddhartha had a retinue of sixty thousand consorts. The young prince continued to partake of the worldly life like an immortal god until the age of twenty-nine.

Seeing an old man, a sick man, a corpse, and a humble ascetic in each of the four directions of the palace gates, Siddhartha contemplated the meaning of his life as a king, his retinue of consorts, and the demands of his father. Then, through the power of his previous aspirations, and through the blessings of the Buddha's of the ten directions, he was again moved by the music of liberation, and he decided to depart his royal life. Renouncing his pride and arrogance, the young prince directed his attention single-mindedly towards awakening. Feeling that there was no time to waste, the prince rode off on his horse at midnight.

Siddhartha then cut his hair in front of the teacher Choten Namdag, dressed in saffron colored robes that were gifted to him by the gods, and became a renunciate. He then traveled to the banks of the Nairanjana River where he remained absorbed in all-pervasive meditative concentration for six years. Each day he would eat one seed from a juniper tree and ardently exert himself in extreme ascetic practices. Enduring these austerities, the young mendicant realised how his practices of body and speech were not nurturing the yearnings of his heart. At a moment of utter exhaustion, a young Brahmin's daughter named Legs Tshoma offered him a bowl of sweet rice milk porridge with honey that contained the essential nutrients of milk from a thousand cows. He understood how ascetic practices would not lead him to enlightenment, and how the path to enlightenment is a middle way between extremes. Upon drinking this delicious rice milk, his body was revived and his complexion shone with the luster of a golden shrine.

Having reached the age of thirty-five, the bodhisattva was approaching his realization of enlightenment. Traveling to Bodhgaya in Northern India, he sat beneath the Bodhi Tree. Along the way, he met a grass-seller named Tashi who offered him a batch of kusha grass that was as smooth as peacocks' feathers. Upon arriving in Bodhgaya, the bodhisattva circumambulated the Bodhi Tree three times, placed the tips of the kusha grass facing eastwards, and sat down upon them. Seated like this, he made the steadfast vow that "even if my body withers, if my skin and bones all decompose, I will sit here without moving this body until I attain the enlightenment which takes eons to discover."

The bodhisattva had the thought that if he did not summon the forces of negativity and provocation that he would not be able to attain Buddhahood. He therefore used his psychic abilities to emanate light-rays from between his eyebrows that enticed the wicked devil Mara, and her four minions of terrifying demons. They approached in ferocious appearances, firing countless weapons of terror at the bodhisattva, yet, through radiating loving-kindness, he vanquished each of them.

The demons then threatened him, telling the bodhisattva that he could not attain liberation because he had not accumulated sufficient merit. The goddess of Earth along with her retinue then proclaimed their witness to the bodhisattva's actions, assuring the demons that he had accomplished and perfected the two accumulations during incalculable eons in the past.[13] Again, the demons appeared in disguise as sexy apparitions who tried to seduce the bodhisattva with their various playful techniques and flirtatious means, but not even one hair moved on his body. Once the bodhisattva conquered this final temptation, the hordes of demons

---

13   The two accumulations (*tshogs gnyis*) are merit and wisdom.

vanished. During dawn of the next morning, Siddhartha overcame the subtlest cognitive obscurations in a state of adamantine meditative stabilization, and actualized complete enlightenment.

In order to demonstrate the profundity of his realization, the Buddha chose not to teach for the period of seven weeks. The world renowned lord of gods Brahma visited the Buddha during this time and offered him a golden wheel with one thousand spokes, and the god Indra offered him a conch-shell trumpet that coiled to the right. Both urgently requested that he turn the Wheel of the Dharma, and teach as he had promised he would before becoming a Buddha.

Eventually, he made his way to the Deer Park in Varanasi where he met his first five disciples. Then on the fourth day of the sixth month of the Tibetan lunar calendar, the Buddha turned the Wheel of Dharma, teaching the Four Noble Truths.[14] Upon hearing this teaching, his five disciples attained the state of an arhat, and the meaning of the Three Precious Gems was first heard in this world.[15]

At the age of thirty-five, Shakyamuni became a fully realised Buddha. Until his passing away, the Buddha held forty-five summer retreats and turned the Wheel of Dharma an innumerable amount of times, explicating teachings on both definitive as well as provisional meanings. Shakyamuni taught in accessible places like Rajagriha, Vulture Peak Mountain, and Vaishali in Northern India, and he taught in trans-worldly places for the gods and other-worldly beings. Through his miraculous abilities, the Buddha manifested himself in incomprehensible places such as the Precious Vajra Palace, and the peak of Mount Sumeru.[16] In places such as these, the Buddha displayed exceptional means for maturing his disciples along their spiritual paths of progression. Present during these assemblies were the Buddha's closest disciples Shariputra and Maudgalyayana along with bodhisattva monks, nuns, laymen, and laywomen. Exemplifying transience and inspiring renunciation in those disciples who cling to the extreme of things

---

14 See glossary for "Four Noble Truths."
15 See glossary for "Arhat" and "Three Precious Gems."
16 Mount Sumeru is the cosmological mountain situated in the center of our world-system. It is surrounded by four continents of which the Southern continent is Jambudvipa, our world.

lasting, in the city of Kushinagar between a pair of sala trees, the Buddha lied down on his right side, placed one foot on the other, and gave his final teaching in his physical form by passing into unexcelled nirvana.

BUDDHISM IN INDIA AFTER THE BUDDHA

The relationships and places where the Buddha resided are recorded in the *Great Treasury of Detailed Explanation*.[17] Translated from the Tibetan translation, it reads,

> Saketa, Vaishali, White Earth, and in the realm of the gods,
> Where the naïve die, Koshambhai, near highland mountain stupas,
> In noisy surrounds, bamboo villages, and in the city of Kapilavastu,
> Buddha spent a year in these places teaching the dharma to the
> fortunate.
>
> Twenty-three years were spent in the city of Shravasti,
> Four years were lived in the Medicinal Forest,
> Two years were in the innermost Barma Cave,
> Five years were in the royal city of Rajagriha,
> Six years were enduring ascetic austerities,
> Twenty-nine years were spent in the palace.
>
> At the age of eighty, the victorious one
> Is known to have passed completely into nirvana.

Some of these places such as Rajagriha, the Nairanjana River where he performed his ascetic practices, the city of Kapilavastu, the city of Rajagriha, and a few of the other places are well-known today while many of these places have become unrecognizable with the changing of time.

In the city of Rajagriha, a year following the Buddha's nirvana, his disciple Mahakashyapa held a council for the compilation of the Buddha's

---

17   Tibetan title: *bye brag bshad mdzod chen mo.*

teachings on the monastic ethical codes or *Vinaya-pitaka* while his disciple Ananda held a council for the compilation of the Buddha's discourses or *Sutra-pitaka*.[18] Mahakashyapa then gathered together all of the Buddha's teachings on both the inner and outer sciences and compiled these into the *Abhidharma-pitaka* collection. Today, we are extremely fortunate to have these *Three Collections* as records of what the Buddha taught according to this First Council.

After Mahakashyapa, these collections were maintained by Ananda, and then Arya Sanavasin, Arya Upagupta, Arya Dhitika, Arya Krsna, and Arya Mahasudarshana. This succession of seven arhats is well-known and cited within the *Minor Precepts of the Vinaya* as well as the *White Lotus Sutra*.[19] Each of these seven arhats maintained the Buddha's teachings very much like the Buddha. Once these seven had passed, the teachings of the Buddha were entrusted to many different arhat monks who were not able to maintain the Buddhist tradition in the same way as this great succession of seven.

One hundred and ten years after the Buddha's nirvana, monks began to behave in ways that were contradictory to the monastic code. As a consequence, a Second Council was held in Vaishali. This Second Council was headed by the arhat Kirti and was attended by seven hundred arhats who had succeeded in the lineage of Ananda. The monks that gathered in Vaishali held a ceremony to purify and restore their vows. They then celebrated this auspicious occasion with a feast.

One hundred and thirty-eight years after the Buddha passed away, many of the Buddhist monks began to hold different views, and consequently, eighteen distinct shravaka schools were formulated. During the first century B.C., King Kanika invited and sponsored five hundred arhats including Arya Tsiblog, four hundred bodhisattva's including Vasumitra, and an excessive amount of ordinary practitioners who upheld the *Three Collections* of the Buddha's teachings to Nagyan Temple in Kashmir. As it was foretold in the *Sutra of King Krikin's Prophetic Dreams*, each of these eighteen schools followed the authentic words of the Buddha, and decisively recorded previous-

---

18   See glossary for "Vinaya-pitaka" and "Sutra-pitaka."
19   Tibetan title: *snying rje pad dkar po'i mdo.*

ly unwritten accounts, accurately arranging the collections of the Buddha's teachings.[20] These revisions and corrections comprised the Third Council.

As for the extraordinary Mahayana collections of teachings, hundreds of thousands of bodhisattvas gathered on the southern Vimasambhava Mountain in the city of Rajagriha, the ancient capital of Magadha. There, Manjushri taught the Abhidharma or inner and outer sciences, Maitreya taught the Vinaya or ethical codes of conduct, and Vajrapani taught the Sutras or sets of the Buddha's discourses. The great Indian master Bhavaviveka also proclaimed in his *Blaze of Reasoning* that the Mahayana was taught by the Buddha, and that its primary texts were compiled by Samantabhadra and Maitreya.[21] However this may be, it is not clear exactly when a Mahayana Council took place.

After the Buddha's nirvana, many disagreements arose amongst the ordained within the Buddhist community about which spiritual approach to follow. The majority of monks decided to adhere to the Hinayana or shraka approach, and as a consequence, the Mahayana teachings degenerated. This period lasted until the charismatic figure Arya Nagarjuna, and his disciples appeared in the first century C.E. Then, a few hundred years later, by the time of Asanga and Vasubandhu, the philosophy of the Mahayana was revived and had become wide-spread.

Nagarjuna's lineage of spiritual sons that upheld the Madhyamaka philosophy include the master Aryadeva, the master Buddhapalita, the master Bhavaviveka, the great learned Shantarakshita, and the master Shantideva. The lineage of spiritual sons that succeeded Asanga include his younger brother Vasubhandu, Arya Namdrolde, the revered Gunaprabha, master Dignaga, the master Lodro Tenpa, Dharmakirti, the master Chandragomin, and the master Shakyaprabha. While Nagarjuna, Asanga, and Dignaga are known as the authors of fundamental Buddhist philosophical texts, Aryadeva, Vasubandhu, and Dharmakirti are known as the authoritative commentators. Together, they are known as the Six Ornaments that adorn our world. Gunaprabha and Shakyaprabha are known as the Two

---

20 Tibetan title: *rgyal po kri kri'i rmi lam lung bstan pa'i mdo*.
21 Tibetan title: *rtog ge 'bar ba*.

Supreme Masters because they helped to spread the ethical codes within the Vinaya that serve as the basis for the Buddha's teachings.

Shantideva and Chandragomin contributed immensely towards the flourishing of Buddhism in India, and for this reason they are referred to as the Two Marvelous Masters. Shantideva was a great scholar at Nalanda Monastic University, and when some of his colleagues tested his knowledge, he uttered his famous composition, *Entering the Bodhisattva's Way of Life*.[22] As he taught the chapter on wisdom, he began to explain "the tangible and the intangible...," magically lifting off the ground into the sky. Continuing to elucidate to the crowd, his body disappeared and only his voice was heard. At the age of seven, Chandragomin became famous for defeating non-Buddhists in debate, and while he was visiting Nalanda University, praising a stone Manjushri statue, the statue turned its face and gazed at him.

Besides these great spiritual teachers, there were the six famous scholars of the six gates of Vikramalashila Monastery. Guarding the eastern gate was the all-knowing Ratnakarnashanti, guarding the southern gate was Prajnakaramati, guarding the western gate was Manjushri, guarding the northern gate was Naropa, the first central pillar was attended by the Brahmin Ratnavajra, and the second pillar was attended by Jnanamitra. In fact, there were many hundreds of accomplished Buddhist scholars and yogis living in India at that time. As the history of India reflects, Buddhist communities were so prevalent that it is difficult to estimate how many there were.

Generally, the secret Vajrayana or Buddhist tantric teachings are thought to have been taught by the Buddha after his Third Turning of the Dharma Wheel.[23] These teachings were initially set forth for King Indrabodhi in

---

22 Tibetan title: *byang chub sems dpa'i spyod pa la 'jug pa*.
23 The Third Turning of the Dharma Wheel is the third of the Three Successive Turnings of the Dharma Wheel (*bka' 'khor lo rim pa gsum*). These turnings or revolutions are: 1) the First Turning which encompasses the Four Noble Truths, and the teachings on interdependent origination; 2) the Second Turning which encompasses the *Transcendent Wisdom Scriptures* or *Prajnaparamita Sutras*, and the teachings of Madhyamaka; 3) the Third Turning which encompasses the teachings on Buddha-nature, and the luminous nature of mind. Teachings of "definitive meaning" (*nges don*) are in contrast to teachings of "provisional meaning" (*drang don*); this is a reference to Buddhist interpretive schemas for determining which of the Buddha's words and their subsequent commentaries express the ultimate intent of the Buddha.

Uddiyana, a country which is believed to be in the vicinity of present-day Pakistan. King Indrabodhi, his queen and their attendants transcended to wisdom-holders or beings who have realised the meaning of tantra through practice. Because all of the children in this city became tantric adepts, and were able to fly through the sky, Uddiyana became renowned as the "Home of Sky-Dancers." The tantric lineage of King Indrabodhi continues to be transmitted through wisdom-holder masters up to today.

In particular, the *Kalachakra Tantra* was taught by the Buddha at Dre-pung or White Rice Mount in the south of India to the Buddhist King Suchandra, and his entourage. Since then, the *Kalachakra Tantra* has been a primary practice of great emanatory Dharma Kings. In both India and Tibet, many accomplished scholars and yogis have held this tantra in the depths of their hearts, and now the *Kalachakra* has flourished in our world. These days the *Kalachakra* is considered by practitioners of both the Early and Later Translation Traditions to be one of the most efficient means to enlightenment amongst all of the tantras.

CHAPTER IV

THE NYINGMA TRADITION

EARLY TRANSLATIONS AND THE FLOURISHING OF TIBETAN BUDDHISM

The Transmission of Buddhism into Tibet

Although the Buddha's teachings flourished in India, the continuity of Indian Buddhism was interrupted due to the destruction of invading barbarians. One famous incident in the destruction of Buddhism in India was when the beggar Suryasiddhi set Nalanda Monastic University ablaze because he did not care for some of the delinquent behavior of a few of the Buddhist monks there. Because several similar unfortunate circumstances occurred, Buddhism in India fell into a state of extreme degradation. This was prophesized by the Buddha in his *Immaculate Goddess Sutra*.[24]

Due to the kindness of the bodhisattva Tibetan Kings, ministers, scholars, and translators, the complete lineages of explanation and realization of the Buddha's Hinayana, Mahayana, and Vajrayana teachings were flawlessly transmitted into Tibet. Even after the Red Army's severe destruction of the symbolic representations of Buddhism such as monasteries, temples, and reliquaries of the Three Jewels, and after the diaspora of the Tibetan people,

---

24 Tibetan title: *lha mo dri ma med pa'i mdo.*

Buddhism in Tibet remains largely unimpaired. This is undoubtedly due to the kindness of the lineage-holders who have sustained the Tibetan Buddhist traditions of explanation and realization.

In particular, many lamas and tulkus who uphold the nonsectarian Rimed Buddhist tradition of philosophy and practice escaped into India, Nepal, Bhutan, and many Western countries after Tibet lost her independence, and the Fourteenth Dalai Lama fled into exile in 1959. Consequently, the Tibetan refugee community has upheld, preserved, and spread the precious teachings of the Buddha in exile. As a result, Tibetan Buddhism is known in many countries throughout the world and is becoming more well-known every year.

Moreover, it is not that Buddhism just naturally took root in Tibet, it took generations of sacrifice and concerted effort in order to transplant the Buddha's teachings into the Land of Snow. Thankfully, due to the intense respect, devotion, and perseverance of the Tibetan people, the conditions were created for the flourishing of Buddhism in Tibet. As the various instructions of Indian scholars and adepts were put into practice, the Tibetan people deepened their understanding of these instructions, and Buddhism eventually became more and more supported. Because certain individuals began to hold distinct lineages, and because their disciples successively adhered to particular systems of thought and practice, there arose different traditions of Tibetan Buddhism. Without considering their differences, it is important to know that the views of all of these traditions are entirely reliant upon the model of base, path, and fruition. For example, although we eat different foods that have different flavors, all the foods we eat are for the sole purpose of nourishing our bodies.

There are the more widely disseminated and known traditions of Tibetan Buddhism such as the Nyingma, Kagyu, Sakya, Jonang, Zhijed, Shalupa, Podongpa, Geluk, and then there are many other traditions that faded through time. Nowadays, there are five traditions that have taken root, and have maintained their autonomous philosophical systems and meditation practices through building monasteries, and training lineage-holders to uphold their distinctive tradition. These are the Nyingma, Kagyu, Sakya,

Jonang, and the Geluk. They can be called the five great traditions of Tibetan Buddhism.

The lineage accounts, views, and practices of these traditions are concisely described and distinguished according to their philosophical views and their tantric systems. That is, if they are of the *zhentong* or *rangtong* Madhyamaka tradition, or if they are of the Early or Later Translation Traditions of the tantras. If they are of the Early Translation Tradition then they are referred to as "Nyingma," and if they are of the Later Translation Traditions then they are referred to as "Sarma." These are the major ways in which Buddhism was transmitted into Tibet.

The Early Nyingma Tradition

The Nyingma tradition can be traced back to the year 433 C.E. when the first Buddhist scriptures were brought into Tibet during the reign of King Latho Thothori Nyentsan. Then, during the seventh century, Buddhism was formally introduced into Tibet by King Songtsen Gampo (d. 650). During the eighth through the early ninth centuries, King Trisong Deutsen (790-844) further developed and propagated Buddhism throughout Tibet.

If we begin to count from Nyatri Tsenpo, who is considered to have been the first King of Tibet, King Latho Thothori Nyentsan was the twenty-eighth Tibetan King. During King Latho Thothori's reign, a Nepali scholar named Losemtsho, and a translator named Lithese visited him and offered the king a text titled, "The Symbolic Seal that Fulfills what is Witnessed," a golden stupa, and an engraved mould for reproducing wish-fulfilling gems.[25] Even though the king did not know the meaning of these sublime objects, he respected and venerated them. King Latho Thothori went on to live a long and prosperous life, fulfilling his social responsibilities benevolently. More importantly, these gifts were an omen for the future flourishing of Buddhism in Tibet.

---

25 Tibetan title: *dpang skong phyag rgya.*

Later, King Songtsen Gampo sent his minister, the translator Thonmi Sambhota to India where he learned the Gupta script that was used as a template to devise the Tibetan alphabet. The *Cloud of Precious Jewels Sutra*, the *Casket of Mystical Formulations*, and the *White Lotus Sutra* were consequently translated from the Sanskrit into Tibetan along with many other Buddhist texts.[26] During this time, King Sontsen Gampo's minister Gartongtsen, through his diplomatic artistry, invited the Nepali King Amashuvarma's daughter Princess Brikuti to wed King Songtsen Gampo, and become the Queen of Tibet. As royal dowry gifts, the princess brought with her a statue of the Jowo Mikyo Dorje crowned Buddha, a statue of the future Buddha Maitreya turning the Wheel of Dharma, and a self-manifested sandalwood Tara statue.

King Songtsen Gampo and Queen Brikuti also constructed temples in order to further tame and subdue the indigenous forces of danger and opposition. In doing so, they arranged temples in specific locations according to divination, and the geomantic principles of the local districts of Tibet, and the Himalayan region. These temples included the miraculous Tsuglag Khang Temple in Lhasa, Tradrug Temple, Katsal Temple, Tsangdram Temple, Trompa Gyang Temple, Longtang Drolma Temple, Mangyul Jamtrin Temple, and Bumthang Temple in Bhutan. After they completed these district guarding temples, Queen Brikuti visited Othang Lake in Lhasa where she tossed her ring into the air with her wish, and the great Rasa Trulnang Temple magically appeared where her ring landed.

King Songtsen Gampo also married the daughter of the Chinese King Thong Thay Jung, Princess Wun Shing Kongjo. As dowry, the princess brought with her from China a Jowo Shakyamuni Buddha statue. She then built Ramoche Temple in Lhasa to house her precious gift. One of King Songsten Gampo's Tibetan queens, Queen Ruyong Za built a temple at the King's meditation cave Drug Lhalupuk, and another one of his Tibetan queens Mangza Tricham built a temple in Yerwa. Another notable occurrence during the reign of King Songtsen Gampo is that the Brahmin Shan-

---

26   Tibetan titles: *mdo sde dkon mchog sprin, za ma tog gi bzungs, snying rje pad ma dkar po'i mdo.*

kar, the Nepali master Shilamanju, and the great Chinese master Hashang Mahayana arrived in Tibet, and translated many Buddhist texts.

The King, the Abbot, and the Master

During the eighth and early ninth centuries, King Trisong Deutsen (790-844) ruled over Tibet. After considering the Buddhist texts that were translated by his predecessors, and how his forefathers contributed to the dissemination of Buddhism, the King became motivated to spread the sublime teachings of the Buddha throughout Tibet. He first invited the Indian scholar Abbot Shantarakshita who taught the ten virtues and twelve links of interdependence.[27] Though the King and the Abbot thought to lay the foundation of Samye Temple, as they built it, mischievous ghosts and demons interrupted their every attempt. According to prophecy, the King then invited Master Padmasambhava from Uddiyana who bound the ghosts and demons under oath. Samye Temple was then spontaneously constructed without any further disruptions.

King Trisong Deutsen's queens also had temples built near Samye. Queen Lady Changchub Dron constructed the Temple of Abundant Beauty while Queen Lady Margyen of Tsepang had the Copper Temple of the Three Realms built, and Queen Lady Gyalmo Tsun of Phogyong oversaw the construction of the Golden Orphan Temple.[28]

---

27   The ten virtues (*dge ba bcu*) are: 1) refraining from cutting-off life (*srog gcod pa spong pa*); 2) refraining from taking what has not been given (*ma byin par len pa spong ba*); 3) refraining from sexual misconduct (*'dod pas log par g.yem pa spong pa*); 4) refraining from speaking falsely (*brdzun du smra ba spong ba*); 5) refraining from speaking crude words (*tshig rtsub po smra ba spong ba*); 6) refraining from speaking slanderously (*phra mar smra ba spang ba*); 7) refraining from speaking non-sensible words (*tshig bkyal ba smra ba spong ba*); 8) refraining from a covetous mentality (*brnab sems spong ba*); 9) refraining from a malicious mentality (*gnod sems spong ba*); 10) refraining from perverted views (*log par lta ba spong ba*). The twelve links of interdependence (*rten 'brel bcu gnyis*, Skt: *pratityasamutpada*) are: 1) ignorance (*ma rig pa*); 2) propensities (*'du byed*); 3) consciousness (*rnam par shes pa*); 4) name and form (*ming dang gzugs*); 5) six sources of sensation (*skye mched drug*); 6) contact (*reg pa*); 7) sensation (*tshor ba*); 8) craving (*sred pa*); 9) grasping (*nye bar len pa*); 10) becoming (*srid pa*); 11) birth (*skye ba*); 12) decaying and death (*rga zhi*).
28   Gegye Jema Ling (*dge rgyas bye ma gling*) was constructed by Queen Lady Changchub Dron; Khamsum Zangkhang Ling (*khams gsum zangs khang gling*) was constructed by Queen Lady Margyen of Tsepang; Putsab Serkhang Ling (*bu tshab gser khang gling*) was constructed by Queen

The King knew that in order to establish the Buddha's teachings in Tibet, it was imperative that the *Buddhist Canon* be translated into Tibetan. With this long-term vision, he selected and trained young bright Tibetans as translators, and invited the greatest masters from India to teach. These masters included the Kashmiri scholar Jinamitra, the Indian scholar Danashila, and many other important upholders of the Three Collections of Buddhist Scriptures.[29] These scholars, along with the Abbot Shantarakshita, the Master Padmasambhava, the translators Vairochana, Kawa Paltsek, and Chokro Lui Gyaltsen are responsible for translating the most famous of the Buddha's sutra and tantra scriptures along with their commentaries into the Tibetan language. In order to test the Tibetans' abilities to observe the Buddhist monastic precepts, Abbot Shantarakshita then selected and ordained seven Tibetan monks. These seven monks served as the first Tibetans to uphold Buddhist monasticism and the Buddhist community in Tibet, and are regarded as the basis for the later flourishing of Buddhism.

The translator Vairochana and the Master Padmasambhava's disciple Namkhai Nyingpo were then sent to India to study and receive transmissions. Vairochana studied Dzogchen or the Great Perfection practice with Shri Singha, and Namkhai Nyingpo received teachings on Vishuddha or Wrathful Vajra Deity practice from Hungkara. Both Vairochana and Namkhai Nyingpo became highly accomplished masters before returning to Tibet.

At the King's request, Master Padmasambhava displayed the Eight Mandalas for Accomplishing the Wrathful Deities in the forest charnel ground at Chimpu hermitage above Samye.[30] Later, the King along with his royal

---

Lady Gyalmo Tsun of Phogyong.

29 See glossary for "Tripitaka."

30 The Eight Mandalas for Accomplishing the Wrathful Deities (*sgrub pa bka' brgyad kyi dkyil 'khor*) are the mandalas of the eight principle wrathful meditation deities (Skt: *heruka*) of the Nyingma tradition's Mahayoga class of tantras. These eight mandalas of deities are: 1) Body of Manjushri (*'jam dpal sku*); 2) Lotus Speech (*pad ma gsung*); 3) Perfect Mind (*yang dag thugs*); 4) Quality of Nectar (*bdud rtsi yon tan*); 5) Mystic Dagger Activity (*phur pa phrin las*); 6) Sorcerer Mother (*ma mo rbod gtong*); 7) Cursing Fierce Mantra (*dmod pa drag sngags*); 8) Mundane Praise (*'jig rten mchod stod*).

entourage attained exceptional spiritual powers due to this performance. On other such occasions, at Kharchu in Lhodrak, Shoto Titro in Drigung, and Drakar in Domey, Master Padmasambhava taught the *Unexcelled Tantras*. During these profound teachings, as the Master turned the Wheel of Dharma, his twenty-five main disciples along with crowds that filled the mountainsides attained heightened levels of realization.

The King, the Abbot, and the Master along with the translators, Kawa Paltsek, Chokro Lui Gyaltsen, and Zhang Yeshe De were the forefathers of Buddhism in the Land of Snow. By translating and making available the Buddha's words, and their Indian commentaries, they overcame the negative forces that had prevented the teachings from taking root in Tibet. Their translations of the sutras, tantras, and explanatory texts comprise the Early Translation Tradition, also known as the Nyingma tradition.

The Later Nyingma Tradition

The Nyingma tradition consists of an extended lineage of sequential oral transmissions from the Buddha that were translated during the early translation period, a direct lineage of revealed treasure texts, and a profound cycle of pure visions. These three cycles of teachings comprise the entirety of Nyingma scriptures and guidance instructions. The textual foundations for these ancient cycles of teachings are the oral transmissions of the *Summary of the Meaning of Sutras*, the *Guhyagarbha Mayajala Tantra*, and the eighteen *Dzogchen Tantras*.[31]

The oral transmissions of these cycles were received by Jnana Kumara of Nyag from Padmasambhava, Vimalamitra, Vairochana, and Yudra Nyingpo. In the ninth century, Nubchen Sangye Yeshe and then later Zur Shakya Jungnay received the complete oral transmissions of the Early Translation Tradition, and through their compositions, they

---

31   Tibetan title: *mdo sgyu sems gsum.*

made the teachings of these three principle transmission lineages famous throughout Tibet.[32] With the appearance of the eleventh century translator Rongzom Chokyi Zangpo (1012-88), and the fourteenth century luminary Longchen Rabjam Drimed Odzer (1308-63), the sequential lineage of the secret Vajrayana teachings of the Nyingma reach a new height.

In the year 1159, Kadampa Deshek Sherab Senge (1122-92) founded the great vajra-seat of Kathok Monastery in Eastern Tibet; in 1632, the Dzogchen awareness-holder Ngaki Wangpo (1580-1639) founded Jangter Monastery or Thubten Dorje Drak in Central Tibet; in the year 1665, the great Rigdzin Kunzang Sherab founded Palyul Monastery in Eastern Tibet; in the year 1675, the great treasure revealer Terdak Lingpa (1646-1714) founded Mindro Ling Monastery in Central Tibet; in the year 1684, the great accomplished master Dzogchen Padma Rigdzin (1625-97) founded Dzogchen Monastery in Eastern Tibet; and in the year 1734, the second emanation of Shechen Rabjam, Shechen Gyaltsen Pema Namgyal founded Shechen Monastery in Eastern Tibet. These monastic seats serve as the sources for the great flowing river of the Nyingma. Together they represent the magnificence of the Early Translation Tradition, and how these teachings and practices spread throughout Tibet.

In particular, the sequential lineage of the Nyingma went through a renaissance with the arrival of the great nineteenth century figure Jamgon Mipham Rinpoche. Capturing the intent of both Rongzom Chokyi Zangpo and Longchen Rabjam through his writings, Mipham Rinpoche ascertained the absence of perverted views. Today his works constitute the core of the Nyingma scholastic curriculum, and are considered authoritative for learning both Buddhist as well as non–Buddhist philosophical systems.

---

32 The three principle transmission lineages of the Nyingma or Early Translation (*snga 'gyur*) tradition are: 1) the sequential lineage of the Buddha's words (*ring brgyud bka' ma*); 2) the direct lineage of revealed treasure texts (*nye brgyud gter ma*); 3) the profound lineage of pure visions (*zab mo dag snang*).

VIEWS AND PRACTICES OF THE EARLY TRANSLATION TRADITION

Dzogchen: The Great Perfection

Although an exploration of the elaborate views and practices of the Nyingma's philosophical and meditative systems are beyond the scope of this chapter, I would like to offer a brief introduction to some of the fundamentals derived from the early translation period. To begin with, the Nyingma commentarial tradition bases its entire progression of practices on the *Matrix of Mystery* or *Guhyagarbha Tantra*, and the *Embodiment of Sutras*.[33] Alternatively, the Sarma commentarial tradition bases itself upon the tantric practices of the later translation period which include the Six Yogas, the Five Stages, and the Path and its Result.[34] With this in mind, we can begin to explore the distinctive Dzogchen system of the Nyingma.

Dzogchen is subdivided into the practices of Trekcho or cutting-through to primordial purity, and Thogal, the practice of directly surpassing to spontaneous presence. While the path of Thogal emphasizes instantaneous liberation through the application of effort, Trekcho effortlessly clears away rigidity and resistance so that one's own primordially pure nature radiates forth. Together, these comprise the Dzogchen path of freely resting without effort, and are the main practices of the Nyingma tradition.

In order to proceed with these practices of primordial purity and spontaneous presence, and realize the nature of one's own awareness, it is necessary to receive pointing-out instructions from a qualified teacher. What is known as "Dzogchen" or the "Great Perfection" is one's own unconfined nature. This is innate naked empty awareness, the utter perfection of phenomenal reality that encompasses the vast expanse of samsara and nirvana.

---

33 Tibetan title: *gsang snying dang 'dus mdo*.
34 Tibetan title: *sbyor drug, rim lnga, lam 'bras*. These are three esoteric tantric systems: the Six Yogas are instructions according to the *Kalachakra Tantra*; the Five Stages are instructions from the Father Tantras; the Path and its Result or Lamdre are instructions from the Sakya tradition.

Since the nature of one's own awareness is uncreated, and not fabricated in any way whatsoever, it can remain freely at ease in its natural state. The practice of recognizing the presence or absence of one's discursive movements of mind, without suppressing or defending, accepting or rejecting, is the practice of sustaining naked empty awareness, the marvelous path of Dzogchen.

While the uncommon path of Dzogchen consists of the accumulation of wisdom, the common path consists of practicing the allied forces of loving-kindness and compassion. Moreover, the fruition of Dzogchen meditation is indicated by self-manifesting signs of success that come about through the accumulation of both merit and wisdom. Similarly, the practice through which one sustains these two accumulations culminates with four visions: 1) actualizing the ultimate nature of reality; 2) enriching one's meditative experiences; 3) reaching the full expression of awareness; 4) exhausting the ultimate nature of reality.[35] In addition to these four visions, there are the four levels of a wisdom-holder which are ultimately the realization of the basic universal expanse of phenomena, the indivisibility of samsara and nirvana.[36] The final fruition of this practice is discovery of the kingdom of Samantabhadra, the original Buddha.

Distinctive Traits of Nyingma Practice

One may wonder what the distinctive traits of the uncommon approach of the Nyingma tradition are. In general, all of the traditions of Tibetan Buddhism maintain the specific practices and various guidance instructions from both the sutra perspective, as well as from the perspective of the

---

35   The four visions (*snang bzhi*) of Dzogchen practice are: 1) actualizing the ultimate nature of reality (*chos nyid mgnon sum*); 2) enriching one's meditative experiences (*nyams gong 'phel*); 3) reaching the full expression of awareness (*rig pa tshad phebs*); 4) exhausting the ultimate nature of reality (*chos nyid zad pa*).

36   The four levels of an awareness-holder or vidyadhara (*rig 'dzin rnam pa bzhi go 'phang*) are: 1) the mature wisdom-holder (*rnam smin rig 'dzin*); 2) the life master wisdom-holder (*tshe bang rig 'dzin*); 3) the symbolic seal wisdom-holder (*phyag chen rig 'dzin*); 4) the spontaneous presence wisdom-holder (*lhun grub*).

tantras. For instance, the secret Vajrayana practices of the Sarma or Later Translation Traditions emphasize loosening the knots and bonds of the inner channels, winds, and essences. These practices involve extremely subtle and delicate yogic procedures of communicating with the tantric deities through hand and bodily gestures. In the Nyingma Dzogchen system, if a practitioner knows how to perfectly rest without applying effort, then it is not necessary to deliberately unbind the channels, winds, and essences. This ability to attain realization and traverse the levels of an awareness-holder without performing precise gestures with one's hands and body is a distinctive trait of Dzogchen meditation.

Only if a practitioner is relying on a tantric path that involves techniques for loosening the inner knots within the channels, winds, and essences is it necessary to be guided by the wisdom of great bliss that comes about through relying on an actual female wisdom-consort, or specific symbolic hand and bodily gestures. For an authentic Dzogchen yogi, there is no need to rely on a physical wisdom-consort or the performance of symbolic gestures since the Dzogchen path is ultimately without effort. Nevertheless, tantric Tibetan Buddhist traditions other than the Nyingma rely on physical wisdom-consorts or symbolic gestures in order to expediently reach pinnacle realization. This is to say that the Nyingma have thought physical wisdom-consorts and symbolic gestures to be unnecessary while the Sarma traditions have considered them essential. However, these days, it is permitted and even considered necessary for practitioners of both the Sarma and the Nyingma traditions to have a physical wisdom-consort. This profound factor distinguishes the uncommon tantric approach of the Nyingma from those of the Sarma traditions. For this reason, the techniques for piercing into the vital points of the channels, winds, and essences are very important.

Nyingma and Sarma

In the year 901, the Tibetan King Darma began an enduring persecution of Buddhism, and the Buddhist monastic communities in Central Tibet were destroyed and vanished. Then, in the year 973, the remainders of the old

Nyingma tradition were re-sparked in the lower regions of Eastern and Far Eastern Tibet. Eventually, Buddhism began to spread again in Central Tibet. This re-flaming of Tibetan Buddhism is what is designated as the period of the later propagation and dissemination. After this restoration period, great authors of the Nyingma tradition such as Rongzom Chokyi Zangpo, and translators such as Rinchen Zangpo (957-1055), Ngog Loden Sherab (1059-1109), and Drogmi Lotsawa (993-1050) revived Buddhism in Tibet. The translations and compositions of the various cycles of tantras, commentaries, meditation manuals, and guidance instruction texts from this period form what is known as the "Sarma" or New Translation Traditions.

In the past, Tibetan Buddhism had eight Great Chariots of practice lineages.[37] However, now the general instructions from some of these lineages such as the Kadam and Zhije have not been sustained, and they no longer continue, while others have been assimilated into living traditions. The remaining lineages of the Sarma traditions are the Sakya, Kagyu, Jonang, and Geluk.

Transmissions of the awareness-holder lineage are the heart-nectar of Padmasambhava,

These most sublime instructions liberate the coarse body into the body of light!

Through the great secret six transmissions of the Nyingma,

The divine world of white glaciers is beautified!

---

37   These Eight Great Chariots of Practice Lineages or eight independent traditions of Buddhism that flourished in Tibet are: 1) Nyingma; 2) Kadam; 3) Marpa Kagyu; 4) Shangpa Kagyu; 5) Sakya; 6) Jordruk or Six Yogas; 7) Nyendrub; 8) Zhije and Chod.

CHAPTER V

THE SAKYA TRADITION

HISTORY OF THE SAKYA TRADITION

The Founding of Sakya Monastery

Choje Drakpa Gyaltsen wrote about the Sakya,

> White Earth is like the face of a lion,
> Glorious Sakya is the body of this lion.
> Where wishes of the six realms satiate
> Is where Vajradhara resides.

One day while the venerable Tivamkara was walking along the roadside in Tibet, he saw two wild yaks on Ponpori Mountain, and predicted that in the future these yaks would become two Mahakala protectors who would perform fantastic enlightened activities. He then prostrated, and made offerings for the enrichment of the white Earth in this area. Noticing one "Hri" syllable, seven "Dhi" syllables, and one "Hum" syllable etched onto the mountainside, Tivamkara prophesized that one manifestation of Avalokiteshvara, seven manifestations of Manjushri, and one manifestation of Vajrapani would appear in this area in order to tremendously benefit beings.

There was a lineage-holder of the Nyingma secret tantra tradition named Khon Shakya Lodro who had two suns like the sun and the moon. His elder son was Sherab Tsultrim, and his younger son was Khon Konchok Gyalpo (1034-1102). As Khon Konchok Gyalpo was watching a dance performance in Drolung, he had a vision of the various masks of the twenty-eight Shvara goddesses. Since it was considered improper to disclose the secret tantric tradition of the Nyingma, he was advised to study the tantras of the Sarma or Later Translations. He studied the various classes of the new tantras from Drogmi Lotsawa and Gokhukpa Lhatse, and became a very learned and realised master. Then in 1073, at the age of forty, on a mountainside known as "Labonpo" which has features that resemble a sleeping elephant with white Earth shaped like the face of a lion on its right shoulder, Khon Konchok Gyalpo constructed the great monastery of Sakya. Since the establishment of this monastery, the lineage-holders and practitioners from this place have referred to their tradition as "Sakya," literally meaning "White Earth."

Sakya Lineage Masters

At the age of fifty-nine, Khon Konchok Gyalpo had a second wife who gave birth to their son Sachen Kunga Nyingpo (1092-1158). Once Khon Konchok Gyaltsen passed away, because his son was too young to inherit the family lineage, Lotsawa Rinchen Drag assumed leadership of Sakya for nine years. As a youth Jetsun Kunga Nyingpo possessed unusual qualities for a child and was adored by everyone. He received many teachings from his father while he was alive, and he received guidance instructions on the practice of Parting from the Four Attachments from a vision of Manjushri while meditating in a six month retreat. These instructions allowed him to suddenly understand all of the essential points along the path of the Transcendent Wisdom or Prajnaparamita vehicle. Eventually, he became the third successor of Sakya Monastery, and renowned as one of the great Sakya lineage masters.

Kunga Nyingpo attained a high level of realization along the paths and stages of spiritual development, and left a deep impression on the later Sakya tradition. He also had three sons, the oldest being Sonam Tsemo (1142-82), then Drakpa Gyaltsen (1147-1216), and Palchen Odpo (b. 1150). Kunga Nyingpo's youngest son, Palchen Odpo had two sons, the oldest being Sakya Pandita Kunga Gyaltsen (1182-1251) who was the first famous Tibetan pandita.

Sakya Pandita excelled in his studies of the ocean-like scriptural traditions of both Buddhist as well as non-Buddhist philosophical systems, and at the age of twenty-seven was ordained by the Kashmiri Pandita Shakya Shri at Nyangtod Gyangon Temple. He spent his life spreading the teachings of the Buddha not only throughout Tibet, but throughout Mongolia as well. As one of the greatest scholars of Tibet, he is known for having maintained the Buddhist teachings, and for having defeated Hindu extremists in debate who upheld the belief in an all-mighty creator god. Though he composed many works, among his most famous are his *Treasury on the Science of Epistemology*, his *Classification of the Three Vows*, and his *Precious Treasury of Eloquent Explanations*.[38] Considering his many achievements, the kindest contribution made by Sakya Pandita was his development of a new tradition for the explanation of the classical Buddhist sciences.

Palchen Odpo then had a son named Zangtsha Sonam Gyaltsen (b. 1235). From the time that he was born Zangtsha Sonam Gyaltsen was regarded as a great protector of beings, and someone who would uphold the sublime teachings of enlightenment. He received and learned the scriptural traditions of both the sutras and tantras from his uncle Sakya Pandita, and went on to attain supreme magical powers. He also spread the teachings of the Buddha throughout Mongolia, and was awarded the title of "Tishri" or "Imperial Master" by the Emperor. While at the Emperor's palace in Mongolia, Zangtsha Sonam Gyaltsen conferred the threefold Vajra Empowerment. The first empowerment so pleased the Emperor that he gave him power over the thirteen throne-holders of Tibet which are both the upper southern and northern regions, Gurmo, Chumig, Shangs, Zhwalude who are the six throne-holders of Tsang, Gyama, Drikung, Tsalwa, Tangspoche,

---

38   Tibetan titles: *tshad ma rigs gter; sdom gsum rab dbye; legs par bshad pa rin po che'i gter.*

Phagmodru, Yazangde who are the six throne-holders of U, and the upper nomadic regions of Taklung. For the second empowerment, the Emperor gave him power over the three provinces of Tibet, and for the third empowerment, he was given colonized regions of China. Since then, the Sakya successors have inherited both political and spiritual power in Tibet.

The five forefathers of the Sakya tradition are Sachen Kunga Nyingpo, Sonam Tsemo, Dragpa Gyaltsen, Sakya Pandita, and Chogyal Phakpa (1235-80). Of these five, Sachen Kunga Nyingpo, Sonam Tsemo, and Dragpa Gyaltsen were all laymen, so they are referred to as the "three whites" while both Sakya Pandita and Chogyal Phakpa were ordained monks, so they are referred to as the "two reds." Khon Konchok Gyalpo initially founded Sakya Monastery, Kunga Nyingpo established the tradition, Sonam Tsemo and Drakpa Gyaltsen developed and spread the tradition, and both Sakya Pandita and his nephew Zangtsha Sonam Gyaltsen won the political and spiritual authority of the tradition.

The Sakya tradition has had many great masters including Kunkhyen Gorampa Sonam Senge (1429-89), Rongton Sheja Kunrig (1367-1449), Yaktruk Senge Pal, Remdawa Shonu Lodro, Chim Jamyang, Tsonang Sherab Zangpo, as well as many others. These scholars and realised adepts are comparable to the great Buddhist masters of India such as the Six Ornaments and the Two Excellences, and they have all greatly contributed to the flourishing of the Buddha's teachings in every direction.

VIEWS AND PRACTICES OF THE SAKYA TRADITION

The Lamdre Sutra Approach

To begin with, Jamgon Sakya Pandita and Rongton Sheja Kunrig mainly upheld the philosophical view of Svatantrika Madhyamaka. However, Jetsun Remdawa Shonu Lodro upheld the position of the Prasangika Madhyamaka view. Nowadays many Sakya masters when explaining the philosophical position of the Lamdre or Path and its Result agree that the view is simply free from constructions.

The first phase of practicing the path is comprised of learning how to reverse and refrain from non-virtues through understanding how difficult it is to find the freedoms and opportunities of a precious human life, recognizing the infallibility of cause and effect, knowing the defects of samsara, and cultivating loving-kindness and compassion. The next phase consists of overcoming the belief in an enduring self. In order to do this, a practitioner identifies how the mind fixates on the five constituents of an individual and holds these constituents as being truly existent. For instance, if the constituents of an autonomous person were inherently real, then these different constituents could exist without depending upon causes or conditions. Since it is easy to understand that an individual's mind and body are composed of various influences and factors, and since they are made from causes and conditions, it is possible to understand how they lack intrinsic existence.

In this way, a practitioner contemplates over and over again in order to ascertain how the five constituents of an individual arise from causes and conditions, and how the individual person therefore lacks intrinsic or true existence. By recognizing how all phenomena lack true existence, one comes to an understanding of the sublime nature of phenomenal reality. This ultimate lack of true existence is the mind's natural state of emptiness. It is the dissolution of the fabrications of thought. Regardless of beliefs in how things exist or do not exist, how things are or are not, whatever discursive thoughts may occur, because there is no reference or support, there are no distinguishing traits or fabrications of the mind which can be fixated upon. This is how a practitioner progresses along the path of meditation according to the approach of the sutra teachings.

The Lamdre Tantra Approach

To briefly explain the Lamdre path of meditation from the perspective of tantra: a practitioner will initially search over and over again for internal aspects of one's dispositions and capacities of mind. Then, if one examines thoroughly, nothing will be found. This is because the luminous awareness of mind is merely movement, comprehension, clarity, and intelligence. Seeing this single aspect of mind is known as perceiving the empty nature of mind. When experiencing the emptiness of mind, a practitioner looks directly into the empty nature of mind which is not a state of nothingness or vacuity, but is rather naked clarity and awareness. Recognizing how both clarity and emptiness coalesce and mingle inseparably within the luminous nature of awareness is called the "common introduction."

The uncommon introduction is recognition of one's own genuine connate pristine awareness. This is not one's ordinary awareness or simply the mind's delusory perceptions, but is rather recognition of the mind's non-delusory coalescence of emptiness and luminosity at the time of its base. Within sutras and tantras this is referred to as "the complete purification of mind," "Buddhanature," "the mind's natural luminosity," "the adamantine mind," "the continuum of the all-ground," or "the universal basis of awareness." Although beings have been intimately associated with the non-delusory quality of their minds since beginningless time, they have not recognized this. Through an introduction, there is recognition of awareness's coalescence of connate luminous emptiness. This experience of resting in equanimity free from fixations or anything on which to fixate upon is known as the "path of the inseparability of samsara and nirvana."

Accordingly, there are three essential points for acquiring the view. The first is to ascertain how the appearances and references of the mind are constructed, and establish through scriptures and reasoning how the mind's ignorance creates every appearance of external phenomena. Next is to ascertain through examples and logical postulations how every appearance of external phenomena cannot be established as truly existing, and how the mind's internal nature is empty by meditating upon the nature of emptiness. Finally, the third point is to ascertain how existence is produced due to perverted ideas about how reality is truly existent. This leads to a realization of how both the one who fixates and the objects of fixation lack intrinsic existence, and how awareness arises through interdependence on all conditioned phenomena.

What is conditioned is devoid of true or intrinsic existence. Likewise, what is unconditioned must lack intrinsic existence. Since there is nothing which is not dependent upon the conditioned, and since there is not even a facet of the unconditioned which is not dependent upon the conditioned, both the conditioned and the unconditioned are imputations on emptiness. This is said to be awareness of interconnectivity, the view of how samsara and nirvana are inseparable and free from the two extremes.[39] Infallible recognition of reality in this way is inexpressible as this final resolution of the view is beyond thought.

This is a brief explanation of the uncommon view and practice of the Sakya tradition. With this in mind, it is important to know that there is not even the slightest difference in the practices of renunciation and generating the mind of awakening among the various Tibetan Buddhist traditions, just as there is no difference in their ultimate fruition.

The vajra gaze of scriptures and reasoning

This is what destroys the rocky mountains of perverted views!

The glorious Sakya has seized the seal that signifies the Buddha's teachings,

And the decree of both the spiritual and temporal traditions in the cool land of Tibet!

---

39   The two extremes (*mtha' gnyis*) are the extreme of absolutism (*rtag mtha'*) or the view that things truly exist, and the extreme of nihilism (*chad mtha'*) or the view that nothing truly exists.

CHAPTER VI

THE KAGYU TRADITION

HISTORY OF THE KAGYU TRADITION

Marpa, Milarepa, and Gampopa

Marpa Lotsawa, Jetsun Milarepa, and Dakpo Gampopa are known as the three spiritual forefathers of the Kagyu tradition. Dakpo Rinpoche, otherwise known as Gampopa (1079-1153), first received oral guidance instructions from the Kadampa tradition directly from his master Jetsun Milarepa (1040-1123), and he later received transmission of the Mahamudra or Symbolic Seal teachings. The name of the lineage that has sustained the practical guidance instructions which combine these Kadampa teachings with Mahamudra meditation has become known as the Kagyu tradition. Although the instructions of the Kagyu tradition are traced back to the Tibetan translator Marpa Chokyi Lodro (1012-97), the actual name of the tradition is derived from the time of Dakpo Lhaje Gampopa.

Marpa Lotsawa was born in the year 1012 in the Lhodrak region of Southern Tibet. As a child, Marpa studied Sanskrit from Drogmi Lotsawa (993-1050), and he later traveled to India on three occasions in order to meet with scholars and realised masters, and to study with teachers such as the Kashmiri Pandita Jnana Akarala. In particular, he studied with and delighted his master, the great siddha Naropa in three ways.[40] Like a vase filled to its brim, Marpa became full with the teachings that he received from Naropa. It was prophesized that he would raise the victory-banner and establish a tradition in the northern land of Tibet.

In the Flower Adornment City, while bestowing the Hevajra empowerment, the great yogi Naropa manifested the actual Hevajra mandala of deities, and asked his spiritual son Marpa whom he would like to receive the empowerment from, either the deity itself or his root teacher. Marpa thought that he would like to receive the empowerment from the deity first, and later from his teacher, so he requested that the deity perform the empowerment. Naropa then shrunk the mandala into his heart-center, and said to his disciple Marpa that nobody is more important than one's root teacher, as it is one's teacher that is the source of all blessings.

While bestowing the Hevajra empowerment, Naropa told Marpa that his lineage of spiritual successors would last long, and have many great descendents while his family's lineage would soon die out. Although Marpa had one son named Dharma Dodey who died at a young age, the Kagyu tradition continues on to today. Marpa Chokyi Lodro's four main heart-sons were Ngogton Chokyi Dorje from Zhung, Tsulton Wangnge from Dol, Meton Tsonpo from Tsangrong, and Milarepa from Gungthang. As Naropa had prophesized, Marpa did have a son like the sun named Jetsun Milarepa, a son like the moon named Rechung Dorje Drakpa (1083-1161), and sons like the stars such as Ngan Dzongtonpa Changchub Gyalpo.

Jetsun Milarepa was born in the year 1040 in Tsangskya Ngatsa. When he was a child, his father died and he was entrusted to his uncle and aunt where he faced tremendous hardships. Later in his life, his mother sent him to study black magic with the sorcerers Tsangrong Ngar and Nubs Khulung, and after he had vanquished his mother's personal enemies, he met his teacher Marpa. In order to purify his obscurations, Marpa had Milarepa perform countless difficult tasks such as carrying stones on his back for long distances and constructing and then deconstructing towers. Milarepa car-

---

40 Three ways of delighting (*mnyes pa gsum*) one's spiritual teacher are: 1) through one's spiritual practice; 2) through serving one's teacher; 3) through offering material things.

ried out these tasks and was able to perfectly understand the instructions of Marpa. Later in his life, Milarepa wandered Tibet in order to spread the teachings that he had learned, and during his lifetime he was able to actualize the unified state of Vajradhara.

Dakpo Lhaje Gampopa was born in the year 1079. As a young man he studied the Buddhist scriptural tradition, and became an expert in the science of medicine. He married, and when his wife died at an early age, Gampopa decided to renounce the worldly life and become a monk. After taking monastic vows from Loden Sherab, he was moved by hearing of the reputation of Milarepa and as immeasurable devotion arose within him, Gampopa began to seek out this famed yogi. Through receiving the complete guidance instructions on the oral lineage from Milarepa, exceptional experiences and realizations emerged within Gampopa. As Milarepa prophesized, Gampopa went on to reside at Darji Riwo Monastery where he composed many treatises and fulfilled enlightened activities that have greatly contributed to the flourishing of Buddhism in Tibet.

Monasteries and Sub-Lineages

Marpa's monastery is in the Trowo valley of Lhodrak. Marpa's disciple Lama Ngakpa, and Dakpo Gampopa founded the earliest Kagyu monasteries. One of Gampopa's three main disciples, Phagmo Drupa Dorje Gyalpo (1110-70) established the monastery of Dhensa Thil Monastery in Lhoka, Southern Tibet.[41] At the age of eighty, the First Karmapa, Dusum Khyenpa (1110-93) established Tsurphu Monastery in the Tolung valley of Central Tibet, and this continues to be the main monastic seat of the Karmapa's in Tibet.

In addition to these monastic complexes, the Kagyu tradition is subdivided according to various lineages. Dakpo Gampopa's primary disciple, Dusum Khyenpa was the first in the Karmapa lineage of successive rein-

---

41 Jamphal Lodro writes, "Phagmo Drupa is known for having gained both secular and spiritual authority in Tibet."

carnations. Gampopa's disciples Phagmo Drupa, Barom Darma Wang-chuk and Zhang Droway Gonpo Yudragpa who was the disciple of Gam-popa's disciple Gompa Tsultrim Nyingpo each initiated their own major sub-lineages of the Kagyu, and these are known as the Four Great Kagyu Lineages. Taklung Tangpa Tashi Pal (1142-1210), Ling Repa Padma Dorje (1128-88), Trophu Gyaltshab Rinpoche, Zara Kaldan Yeshe Senge, Mar-wa Drubthob Sherab Yeshe, Yerwa Drubthob Yeshe Tsegpa, and Nyamed Gyergom Chenpo established the eight minor sub-lineages of the Kagyu. The great learned and realised Khyungpo Naljor (1002-64) traveled to In-dia where he received signs and visions of tantric deities along with guid-ance instructions on the Six Yogas of Naropa. He later built a monastery in the Yeru district, his lineage of teachings which are known as the Shangpa Kagyu spread throughout Tibet. Both this Shangpa Kagyu along with the Marpa Kagyu are the two great lineages of transmission within the Kagyu tradition.

VIEWS AND PRACTICES OF THE KAGYU TRADITION

The View of Mahamudra

In general, there are no major differences among the views and practices of the various lineages of the Kagyu tradition. Nevertheless, there have been in-stances of individual philosophical systems being set forth through the impar-tial processes of refuting another's position, establishing one's own position, and responding to the criticisms about one's own position. This has led to the articulation of distinctive views within the Kagyu tradition. However, these refutations, establishments, and responses have not created severe sectarian divisions, and even words of partiality composed by the poets and scholars of the tradition sound like eloquent expressions of the nature of reality.

Actually, during the time of meditation, there are no major distinctions among the particular philosophical systems upheld by each of the five different Tibetan Buddhist traditions. Though this is so, the extended lineages of these traditions have set-forth slightly different ways of articulating themselves. For instance, the view of Marpa and Milarepa that serves as the source for the Dakpo Kagyu lineage that was developed in India is known as the Prasangika Madhyamaka or Middle Way Consequence view. The qualities and profundity of this view were clearly seen by the yogi Maitripa while he was reflecting on the meaning of reality. This view was then inherited by Marpa and his disciple Milarepa whose songs of realization are harmonious with this Prasangika view.

The view of the sutra tradition is realization of emptiness according to the approach of the Prajnaparamita or Transcendent Wisdom vehicle, and is referred to as "Mahamudra" or the "Symbolic Seal." The writings of Milarepa, Gampopa, Drikung Kyobpa (b. 1770), Ling Repa, Karmapa Dusum Sangye, and many others are in agreement, while others such as the Third Karmapa Rangjung Dorje (1284-1339) asserted the sutra view of *zhentong* or extrinsic emptiness. In particular, the Eighth Karmapa Mikyo Dorje (1507-54) emphasized the *zhentong* view and elaborated upon it in his writings. Because so many in the successive line of Karmapa reincarnations upheld the *zhentong* philosophical view, the Kagyu tradition is regarded as especially adept at articulating *zhentong*. Though subtle nuances on certain crucial points and distinctions of view have been maintained by many of the Kagyu masters, it is difficult to argue that the sutra perspective of the Kagyu tradition is not in accord with the *zhentong* view.

Mahamudra Meditation

It is also appropriate to say that the viewpoint of the secret tantric approach within the Kagyu tradition is Mahamudra. Nowadays, although many Kagyu masters teach the *zhentong* view from the sutra perspective, there is actually no conflict between the *zhentong* view, and the secret tantric Mahamudra view. Very simply, Mahamudra meditation is defined as the process in which the pristine awareness of luminous great bliss is generated, and the vital winds enter, circulate within, and dissolve into the central channel.

This is the innermost essential practice of all the sections of the unexcelled yoga tantras.

In order to meditate precisely in this way, a practitioner must first establish and clarify the natural mind. Once a practitioner rests the mind in single-pointed equanimity, the vital winds will enter, circulate within, and dissolve into the central channel. This will ignite yogic inner heat, induce the four joys, and generate the pristine awareness of great bliss within the natural mind.[42] Through this contemplative experience known as the "Single White Meditation of the Buddha," emptiness and bliss are integrated in union.

Mahamudra meditation has some slight differences in its initial procedure. For instance, some practitioners may recognize their own mind as being internal, external, as coming into existence, as abiding, or as dissipating while resting in equanimity. This moment of total conviction in the natural mind, when nothing is perceived to exist or not exist anywhere is said to be the attainment of the meaning of Mahamudra. As a practitioner vividly rests composed in meditation without cutting-off past thoughts, without allowing present thoughts to remain uncontrived, and without welcoming future thoughts, the naked essence of mind is perceived. This meditative time is the practice of resolving the depths of mind. In addition to this, there is the practice known as "simultaneous self-liberation" in which a practitioner amplifies whatever kinds of discursive thoughts occur, and through continually familiarizing, regards the actual nature of these discursive thoughts as expressions of the ultimate dimension of reality.

The accomplished masters of the Kagyu tradition have also produced an enormous body of contemplative literature based on the tantras and the primary practices of Mahamudra. This literature includes works on topics such as the *Six Cycles of Equal Taste*, Gampopa's *Yoga of Co-emergent Union*, Drigung Jigten Gonpo's (1143–1217) *Fivefold Mahamudra*, and Tsangpa Gyarey's (1161–1211) *Eight Great Instructions*.[43]

---

42   The four joys (*dga' ba bzhi*) are: 1) Joy (*dga' ba*); 2) Supreme Joy (*mchog dga'*); 3) Exceptional Joy (*khyad dga'*); 4) Co-emergent Joy (*lhan skyes kyi dga' ba*).

43   Tibetan titles: *ro snyoms skyor drung, rje sgam po pas lhan cig skyes sbyor, 'bri gung 'jig rten mgon pos lnga ldan, gtsang pa rgya ras pa sogs kyis khrid chen brgyad.*

In accordance with these various guidance instruction texts, the great yogi Naropa said that the two accumulations of merit and wisdom are like the two wheels of a chariot, and without these two accumulations, the basic ground of the natural state of emptiness cannot be realised. A practitioner engages in meditation based upon these instructions and principles, and combines yogic practices such as the Six Yogas of Naropa, and Six Yogas of Neguma with the view of Mahamudra. These meditation practices are marked with various indications of success such as psychological and physical signs, the emergence of bliss suffusing the body, and the gradual dispersion of inner warmth. When these indications occur, a practitioner consults one of the many condensed instruction texts written to guide yogis along the path, and dispel their individual doubts or suspicions.

Learned and realised masters of India, you are the quintessence of wisdom-mind,

Who taught how to accomplish coalescent Mahamudra in a single life!

Protectors and incomparable masters of the Kagyu tradition,

You are the guides into the divine realm of Tibet!

CHAPTER VII

THE JONANG TRADITION

HISTORY OF THE JONANG TRADITION

Transmission of the Jonang Tradition

The Jonang tradition traces its lineage through the master Kunpang Tukje Tsondru (1243-1313), the fifth Tibetan successor in the Dro Kalachakra lineage, who, in the year 1294, at the age of fifty-one, was requested by the living exemplars and students of the Chi, Drag, and Nag regions of Southern Tibet to establish a monastery in Jomonang.[44] From that time onwards, the spiritual tradition that flourished in that area has been referred to as "Jonang." Although Yumo Mikyo Dorje (11th century) has been attributed as the first to establish the view of the Jonang tradition, it is more appropriate to say that Yumowa widely expounded the philosophical system that later became associated with the "Jonang," as the views and practices of this lineage were previously established in India.[45]

---

44   For a biography of Kunpang Tukje Tsondru, see Byang sems rgyal ba ye shes, pp. 64-142. See also Blo gros grags pa, p. 20.

45   For a biography of Yumo Mikyo Dorje, see Byang sems rgyal ba ye shes, pp. 32-35. See also Blo gros grags pa, p. 18.

The source for the transmission of the Jonang lineage is the illustrious Victor Buddha Shakyamuni.[46] The lineage then continues on through the scholars and yogis of India, and the many accomplished Tibetan adepts in the Land of Snow. In accord with the Buddha's Third Turning of the Dharma Wheel, what was passed on through these masters is the intended understanding of his final set of discourses, the ultimate definitive meaning of the Buddha's teachings. These teachings are found within the Buddha Maitreya's *Five Treasures*, such as his *Unexcelled Continuum* and the other treasure texts,[47] and are also explained within Nagarjuna's *Collection of Hymns* and many similar commentarial treatises. In fact, the Buddha prophesized that one thousand years after his passing into nirvana, there would appear a scholar-monk named Asanga who would have an extraordinary talent for commenting upon the provisional as well as the definitive meaning of his teachings. This is why it is said that Arya Asanga was the first to extensively articulate this system of definitive meaning. Asanga was then emulated by his younger brother Vasubandhu, and by later philosophers such as Dignaga, Dharmakirti, and Chandragomin who were the early formulators of the *zhentong* view of extrinsic emptiness upheld through the Great Madhyamaka system of the Jonang tradition.[48]

While Chandrakirti accepted the system of the *rangtong* view of intrinsic emptiness as it is explicitly indicated by Nagarjuna in his *Six Collections of Reasoning*, masters such as Chandragomin upheld the ultimate *zhentong*

---

46   The term "Victor" (*rgyal ba*) is one of the many epithets for the Buddha. It refers to the Buddha as the one who conquered or was victorious over every adversary force that impedes spiritual transformation.

47   The *Five Treasuries* of Maitreya (*byams chos sde nga*) are: 1) *The Ornament of Clear Realization* (Skt: *abhisamaya-lankara, mngon rtogs rgyan*); 2) *The Ornament of Mahayana Discourses* (Skt: *mahayana-sutra-lankara, theg pa chen po mdo sde rgyan*); 3) *Discerning Appearances from Reality* (Skt: *dharma-dharmata-vibhaga, chos dang chos nyid rnam 'byed*); 4) *Discerning the Middle from Extremes* (Skt: *madhyanta-vibhaga, dbus mtha' rnam 'byed*); 5) *The Unexcelled Continuum* (Skt: *uttara-tantra-shastra, rgyud bla ma*).

48   Zhentong (*gzhan stong*) or "Extrinsic Emptiness" refers to the system of teachings that articulate how the ultimate nature of reality is empty of everything other than itself. The *zhentong* teachings are the distinctive philosophical heritage of the Jonang tradition, and are synonymous with the "Great Madhyamaka" (*dbu ma chen po*).

view articulated by Arya Asanga, and sustained by the Great Madhya-maka.[49] These two masters debated furiously at Nalanda University in India for seven years until finally the philosophical position of the *zhentong* view upheld by the scholar Chandragomin was victorious. At that time, a scholar witnessing these debates exclaimed,

> Oh! While the expositions of the Noble Nagarjuna are medicine for some, and poison for others, the expositions of the Invincible Arya Asanga are pure nectar for everyone!

It is said that this later became a popular song that was sung amongst the people of the Indian City of Magadha.

Gradually masters such as Gangameti, Avadhuti or Gawa Drakpa, the Kashmiri Ratnakarashanti, the great powerful yogi Brahman Sajna, and other scholars and yogis upheld the crucial points of this unerring phil-osophical teaching on Buddhanature, the pure lineage of thought that comprises this great tradition.[50] Then, in the middle of the eleventh cen-tury, this system of Great Madhyamaka philosophy was introduced and began to flourish in Tibet. Although by the time of the early transla-tion period, three of Maitreya's *Five Treasures* had been taught, the two most profound elucidations on *zhentong* Madhyamaka were not taught until later. These expositions on the nature of reality were concealed as treasure texts for a short while, and were not disseminated. Later, the great siddha Gangameti revealed these treasures from within a vase inside a stupa. He then taught them to the scholar Gawadrak who passed the

---

49 Rangtong (*rang stong*) or "Intrinsic Emptiness" refers to the system of teachings that articulate how all things are empty of their own intrinsic existence. The *Six Collections of Reasoning (rigs tshogs drug)* by Nagarjuna are divided into seven, they are: 1) *Verses on the Middle Way* (Skt: *madhyamika-karika, dbu ma'i tshig le'ur byas pa*); 2) *The Root Treatise on Wisdom* (Skt: *prajnamula, rtsa ba shes rab*); 3) *The Elegantly Woven Scripture* (Skt: *vaidalya-sutra, zhib mo rnam 'thag*); 4) Reversing the Roots of the Mind (Skt: *vigraha-vyavartani, rtsad ldog*); 5) *Seventy Verses on Emptiness* (Skt: *shunyata-saptali, stong nyid bdun cu pa*); 6) *The Sixty Stanzas on Reasoning* (Skt: *yuki-shastika, rigs pa drug cu ba*); 7) *The Precious Garland* (Skt: *ratnavali, rin chen phreng ba*).

50 For a biography of Avaduti, see Byang sems rgyal ba ye shes, pp. 14–15. Both Avaduti and Sajna are listed as later figures responsible for spreading the Great Madhyamaka Mahayana teachings in India, see Blo gros grags pa, p. 11.

transmission of these teachings onto the great yogi Sajna, who then transmitted them onto the brilliant translator Gaway Dorje, and they were then transferred onto the Tibetan yogi Tsen Kawoche Drimed Sherab, and onto other lineage masters.

From Ngog Loden Sherab (1059-1109) onwards, the transmission of these teachings on the practice and explanation of *zhentong* Madhyamaka became widespread throughout Tibet. From Tsen Kawoche, the lineage was transmitted through Todpa Dharma Tsondru, Dolwa Nya Yeshe Jungnay, Changchub Kyab, Zhonu Changchub, Kyoton Monlam Tsultrim, Chomdan Rigpay Raltri, Kyiton Jampay Dorje, Kunkhyen Dolpopa Sherab Gyalsten, Nyawon Kunga Pal, Gyalsay Choepal Gonpo, Khaidrup Lodro Gyatso, Trulshik Donyod Palzang, Panchen Shakya Chogden, Gyalsay Donyod Drubpa, Jamgon Drubpay Wangpo, Doring Kunga Gyalsten, Khaidrup Lhawang Dragpa, Sangdak Drolway Gonpo, Ngon Chang Rinchen Gyatso, Khaidrup Lodoe Namgyal, Chalung Thinley Namgyal, Ngawang Tenzin Namgyal, Ngawang Khatsun Dargyay, Kunzang Thinley Namgyal, Nudan Lhundrup Gyatso, Tsangtrul Jigme Namgyal, Ngawang Chokyi Phagpa, Ngawang Chojor Gyasto, Ngawang Chophel Gyatsho, Bada Geleg Gyatso, Ngawang Tsoknyi Gyatso, Ngawang Lozang Tsultrim, Dzamngo Kunga Ngawang, Ngawang Lodro Drakpa, and so on up to the living masters.[51]

---

51 Jamphal Lodro writes: "Via these lineage-holders, the sublime scholar and adept, the great yogi Kyabje Lama Ngawang Lozang Thinley received transmission of the Jonang lineage. Lama Ngawang was born in 1917, and through practicing the yoga of Vajrapani became realised. He became fluent in the entire scriptural tradition of both sutra and tantra without studying, and was an expert on the meaning of the yoga of secret mantra Vajrayana. Although he was highly accomplished, Lama Ngawang was content in his life making simple efforts to teach and accumulate merit. His many students including Tulkus and Khenpos are well versed in the *Three Collections of Buddhist Scriptures*. Many of his students are now teaching from the Jonang tradition while others are dedicated to teaching and preserving other Tibetan Buddhist traditions. In 1999, with numerous miraculous signs displayed from his physical body, Lama Ngawang dissolved into the ultimate expanse of reality, promising to reach his faithful students through his compassion and blessings regardless of distance. In particular, there are the closest disciples of this supreme master who are now living in Tibet such as Khenpo Kunga Sherab Saljay, and many other living exemplars of this lineage-holder who are currently teaching the expositions and practices of the Jonang."

The Jonang Kalachakra Lineage

It is understood that the tantras of the secret Vajrayana were taught directly to exceptional disciples in the Akanishta Pure Land, the Heaven of the Thirty-three Gods, on the summit of Mount Sumeru, in the Potala, and other divine realms. It is also said that when the secret Vajrayana was taught personally to the Indian King Indrabodhi, he instantly attained realization. This ultimate realization was then successively transmitted on through male and female yogis to the one-hundredth inheritor, the great master Saraha. These tantric teachings were transmitted to him from the great siddha Shavaripa who received transmission from the glorious protector Noble Nagarjuna. Another lineage of the secret Vajrayana teachings that is commonly accepted among the philosophical schools of Tibet was the transmission passed on from the Buddha manifested as Vajrayogini to Vajrapani, and then onto Jampay Dorje, and so on.

More specifically, the profound teachings of the *Sri Kalachakra Tantra* were requested by the Dharma King Suchandra, and taught by the Buddha Shakyamuni directly to innumerable gods, subterranean serpents, humans, and awareness-holders at glorious Drepung.[52] These teachings were then entrusted to Vajrapani, and King Suchandra later transcribed them, and composed a commentary on the root tantra titled, *Sixty Eight Thousand Verses*. The Kings of Shambhala subsequently composed and promulgated the *Kalachakra Tantra* in the land of Shambhala. By the reign of King Gyalka, the eleventh King of Shambhala, the *Kalachakra Tantra* had existed in Shambhala for about one thousand, eight hundred years.

During this time, as was prophesized, the learned and realised Indian master named Duzhab Chenpo Jampay Dorje had a vision of the bodhisattva of wisdom Manjushri, and of the Shambhala King. One day while walking along, Jampay Dorje encountered an emanation of the King of Shambhala, and during this meeting, he was empowered to practice the *Kalachakra Tantra*. After meditating for six months on the profound yoga

---

52 Drepung was an ancient city in Orissa, India.

of the tantra, Jampay Dorje attained miraculous powers, and was able to transport himself to Shambhala. While there he met with the eleventh King of Shambhala, and received teachings on the *Kalachakra* as well as many other tantras. Some of these teachings he took to heart through memorization, and others he wrote down before returning to India. Upon his return, Jampay Dorje transmitted these tantric teachings to twelve disciples including Duzhab Chungwa and Shribhadra who then passed them onto Bodhibhadra, who transferred them onto the great Kashmiri scholar Dawa Gonpo.

During the eleventh century, Dawa Gonpo traveled three times to Tibet in order to transmit the *Kalachakra Tantra* onto Lama Droton Namseg, Dro Lotsawa Sherab Drakpa, Lama Lhaje Gompa, Drubchen Yumo, and several other qualified recipients. In particular, he bestowed the entirety of empowerments, tantric textual transmissions, and guidance instructions from the *Kalachakra Tantra* on his disciples Dawa Gonpo, and Dro Lotsawa Sherab Drakpa. This initiated the dissemination of the *Kalachakra* teachings in Tibet, and the Dro lineage of the *Kalachakra* sustained by the Jonang tradition. These teachings were then transmitted to the great accomplished yogi Yumo Mikyo Dorje who composed several commentaries on the Six Yogas, and extensively expounded the tantric *zhentong* philosophical system. After Yumo Mikyo Dorje, the lineage was passed on through his heart-son Chokyi Wangchuk, and then Khaypa Namkha Odzer, Machig Tulku Jobum, Khaydrup Namkha Gyalsten, Jamsar Sherab Odzer, Kunkhyen Choku Odzer, Kunpang Thugje Tsondru, and so forth.

The *Kalachakra Tantra* and its related systems were translated into Tibetan by many great translators from the eleventh century onwards. Among the translations of the *Kalachakra Tantra*, and its related systems that spread throughout Tibet, there are two distinct lineages: the Ra lineage and the Dro lineage. While the oral transmissions from the Ra lineage emphasize study, those from the Dro lineage emphasize practice. Accordingly, the Dro lineage upheld by the Jonang tradition is regarded as the most complete.

Origins of the Jonang

One may wonder why the tradition is known as "Jonang." In the Central Tibet province of U-Tsang, in what is nowadays the Lhatse district, there is a place called "Jomonang" inhabited by a queen of the forest named Nag Gyalmo. She is one of the twelve Tenmas or principal female protective deities of Tibet.[53] During the early propagation of the teachings, the master Guru Padmasambhava, Nubchen Namkhai Nyingpo, Dreluay Gyalsten, Nanam Tsultrim Jungnay, and many others came to practice and write in this area. Later, Drogmi Lotsawa, a disciple of the great yogi Konchok attained rainbow-body there. After that, the siddha Darchar Chenpo established a meditation center in that region in order to practice works of both the Early and Later Translation Traditions. Due to yogis having received extraordinary visions of unusual deities in this region, the local people say that this area is endowed with an exceptional capacity for blessings.

In the thirteenth century, Kunpang Tukje Tsondru arrived in Central Tibet and established the monastic complex that later became known as "Jonang." Kunpang Tukje Tsondru, otherwise referred to as Kunpang Chenpo Kuntu Zangpo was born in Tangwachar in the year 1343. He studied at Sakya, Dar, and many other monastic universities in Central Tibet, and became an eminent scholar among even the most learned. From Kunkhyen Choku he received seventeen different empowerments, several tantric transmissions, personal spiritual advice, and guidance instructions on the Six Yogas of the Kalachakra that made him overflow with experiences of realization.

By strengthening his five vital winds through the yoga of harnessing internal life-force energy, the third of the six subsidiary yogas, Tukje Tsondru acquired such exceptional spiritual abilities that he could throw ten people at a time by just touching them with his hand. Because of his ability to harness his vital winds, his attendants would often have to live in the uncom-

---

53   The twelve Tenma female protective deities (*brtan ma bcu gnyis*) are local earth goddesses regarded as guardians of Central Tibet.

fortable extremes of heat and cold that he would create. In fact, during one of his meditations, Tukje Tsondru had a vision of the eleven-headed form of Avalokiteshvara who told him that he was the reincarnation of the siddha Soton Kunrig, and he was then given permission to lift the secret seal and practice the Six Yogas of the *Kalachakra Tantra*. Through his wish to condense the essential intentions of the *Kalachakra Tantra*, he continually recited supplications until one day he had a vision of all of the Kings of Shambhala simultaneously.[54]

The female protector Nag Gyalmo of Jonang then requested Tukje Tsondru to come to Jomonang. Though he declined this request at first, he said that he would come in the future when the time was right. Finally, after the coincidence of certain auspicious circumstances, and after numerous requests from the teachers, students, and spiritual community of the Chi, Drag, and Nag regions, Tukje Tsondru moved to Jomonang. Once he made his residence there, fortunate signs and omens immediately began to occur. He then arranged and recorded all of the existing orally transmitted guidance instructions on the Six Yogas, and as prophesized, he had a vision of the Kalachakra deity. These writings were among the first manuals on the Six Yogas of the *Kalachakra Tantra* in Tibet.

Before his arrival at Jomonang, there were approximately thirty practitioners, and after living at Jomonang for some time, six hundred great meditators of both the Early and Later Translation Traditions resided there. Towards the latter part of his life, the Sakya master Drogon Chogyal lived in Jomonang as well as many other masters who made their home there. After living at Jomonang for twenty-one years, Tukje Tsondru entrusted the monastic complex of Jonang to his disciple Changsem Gyalwa Yeshe Yontan Gyatso (1260-1327), and in the year 1313, passed into the great expanse of reality.

---

54 Jamphal Lodro writes, "While at Kyid Phuk, Tukje Tsondru had a vision of the great Indian siddha Virupa, and was inspired to compose a manual compiling the Path and its Result."

The Omniscient Sherab Gyaltsen

After Yontan Gyatso maintained Jonang Monastery for eight years, the world-renowned scholar and adept Kunkhyen Dolpopa Sherab Gyaltsen (1292-1361) accepted leadership of Jonang. As prophesized about Kunkhyen Dolpopa in *The Large Drum Sutra*,[55]

> In the future, there will appear a youth from a noble family of Magadha who is delightful for the entire world to see, he will be from the Kayori family, and he will become a monk with a name similar to mine.

Also it is prophesized in the *Victorious Crown Tantra*,

> Approximately one-and-a-half thousand years after the Buddha passes into nirvana, in the country of the red-faced people, there will appear a monk who upholds the teachings as I do. By a river, near a garland of magical fruit-bearing trees, in the city of Yi, to the Kayori family, to a father named "Yeshe Wangchuk" and a mother named "Tsultrim Gyanzhe Drag," a child will be born possessing the name "Buddha." He will hoist and wave the victory-banner of my teaching, and blow the conch of Dharma.

As prophesized, Dolpopa was born into the Kayori family in the year 1292. He was ordained by Khenpo Tsultrim Nyingpo, and given the name Sherab Gyaltsen or "Victory Banner of Wisdom," and he later became known as the "Buddha from Dolpo."

Kunkhyen Dolpopa studied and learned the vast ocean-like sutras and tantras from more than thirty of the greatest teachers living in Tibet during his lifetime, including the spiritual master Kyiton Jamyang. He went on a tour of the major monastic universities within the four mountain ranges of Central Tibet, and was given the title "Kunkhyen" or the "Omniscient One" for his reputation of knowing all of the words and

---

55 Tibetan title: *rnga bo che'i mdo.*

their meanings of both the major and minor scriptures without hesitation. Dolpopa was an exemplary scholar, and one of the towering figures in fourteenth-century Tibet.

At the age of thirty, Dolpopa received full ordination from Khenpo Sonam Dragpa, and moved to Jomonang. While meditating in retreat at the Khacho Deden hermitage, realization of the *zhentong* Madhyamaka view first arose within his mind but he refrained from speaking about this for some time. After staying a few years at Jonang Monastery, Dolpopa erected the Great Stupa of Jonang that liberates upon sight. During this time, due to his myriad activities, Kunkhyen Dolpopa appeared in various guises. While some people saw him giving teachings, others witnessed him constructing the Great Stupa. Some people thought that he had manifested three bodies while others swore that he had eight bodies, as it appeared as if he was performing all of his deeds simultaneously. Fortunately, he was assisted by many humans as well as non-human beings in the raising of the Great Stupa of Jonang.[56]

Previously, Kunpang Tukje Tsondru had predicted that "at this hermitage, there will be a son superior to his father, and a grandson superior to his son." Dolpopa remained at Jomonang for seventeen years, sustaining and unfolding the teachings of the Jonang meditation lineage. In particular, he composed many treatises such as his masterpiece, *Mountain Dharma: Ocean of Definitive Meaning*, and extensively explicated the great philosophical tradition of *zhentong* Madhyamaka in the Land of Snow.

Jonang Lineage Masters

Kunkhyen Dolpopa Sherab Gyaltsen had thirteen famous heart-sons including Lotsawa Lodro Pal (1299-1353), Chogle Namgyal (1306-86), Sazang Mati Panchen (1294-1376), and Nyawon Kunga Pal (1285-1379).[57] After Kunkhyen Dolpopa resigned his leadership position, he

---

56 Jamphal Lodro writes: "Later, this stupa was destroyed but it has been restored, and we can see it today."

57 For a discussion of the heart-sons of Dolpopa, see Blo gros grags pa, pp. 32-39.

appointed Lotsawa Lodro Pal, and the leadership of Jonang Monastery continued.

The great early masters of the Jonang lineage were Kunpang Tukje Tsondru, Changsem Gyalwa Yeshe (1247-1320), and Yontan Gyatso. These three masters along with Kunkhyen Dolpopa and his heart-son Chogle Namgyal are known as the Five Forefathers of the Jonang. Chogle Namgyal composed several treatises on *zhentong* Madhyamaka including the greater and lesser *Destroyer of Delusion*.[58] The master of the teachings Nyawon Kunga Pal composed *The Radiant Ornament of Philosophical Systems*, *The Great Commentary on Valid Cognition which Dispels the Darkness of Awareness*, *The Commentary on Wisdom which Dispels the Darkness of Awareness*, and many other texts.[59] Nyawon Kunga Pal had many great disciples who he taught the sequential lineage of the *zhentong* Madhyamaka philosophy to; some of these disciples include Jetsun Redawa, the King of Dharma Jetsun Tsongkhapa, and the great accomplished master Kunga Lodro. Even though there were not many monastic universities in which one could study detailed commentaries on the *Five Volumes of Teachings* that constitute the basic Buddhist studies curriculum in Tibet, it is noticeable that Jetsun Tsongkhapa later quoted his teacher Nyawon Kunga Pal's *Commentary on Wisdom* in his *Golden Garland of Eloquence*.[60]

This lineage of disciples was then sustained by the great accomplished master Kunlo. Later, the great scholar and yogi, the All-Knowing Jetsun Taranatha (1575-1635) whose wisdom equals the Three Manjushris of the Land of Snow, upheld the Jonang oral lineage of transmissions.[61] This sovereign of the Buddha's teachings was born in the year 1575, and at the age of one, repeatedly said, "I am Kunga Drolchok!" At the age of four, he

58 Tibetan title: *'khrul 'joms che chung.*
59 Tibetan titles: *grub mtha' 'od gsal rgyan, rnam 'grel 'grel chen yid kyi mun sel, sher 'grel yid kyi mun sel.*
60 These *Five Volumes of Teachings* (*bka' pod lnga*) constitute the basic Buddhist educational curriculum in Tibet. They are: 1) Pramana or Epistemology (*tshad ma*); 2) Madhyamaka or Middle Way Philosophy (*dbu ma*); 3) Prajnaparamita or Transcendent Wisdom Philosophy (*phar phyin*); 4) Abhidharma or Inner and Outer Sciences (*mngon pa*); 5) Vinaya or Ethics (*'dul ba*). Tibetan title: *legs bshad gser phreng.*
61 The Three Manjushris of Tibet (*'jam dbyangs rnam gsum*) are: Sakya Pandita, Tsongkhapa, and Longchen Rabjam.

was recognized as the reincarnation of the master of the secret teachings, Kunga Drolchok (1507-1566), and was enthroned at Cholung Changtse Monastery. He later encountered the Indian siddha Zhalanatha in a dream who named him "Taranatha."

Taranatha studied all of the scriptural systems of both Buddhist and non-Buddhist philosophies, including the teachings of the greater and lesser vehicles from the learned masters of Indian and Tibet. His accomplishments as a scholar were so glorious that his reputation spread in every direction. In the year 1611, he established Takten Choling Monastery, and composed many treatises and commentaries on various cycles of guidance instructions, contemplative techniques, and practices of both sutra and tantra. Most significantly, he proclaimed the teachings of *zhentong* Madhyamaka like the roar of a great lion. Not only that but Taranatha explained the methods of practicing, and wrote practical instructions for virtually every section of the tantras from the Later Translation Traditions in Tibet. In fact, there was not even a single tantric tradition that he did not hold in the depths of his mind. Even though he never traveled to India, because of his lives as great Indian siddhas such as Nagpopa, he was able to recount his previous lives and compose a *History of Buddhism in India*.[62] Today, this work is regarded as one of the fundamental sources for Indian Buddhist history, and is often referenced by modern Indian historians.

Of all the celebrated exponents of the profound *zhentong* Madhyamaka philosophy in Tibet, Kunkhyen Dolpopa and Taranatha are considered to be the most exalted masters of the lineage. After these two great masters, their spiritual successors spread throughout the three provinces of Tibet, and the Jonang tradition was well-known everywhere. In particular, Jonang monasteries were known for their meditation practice, and they were unrivaled by the other Tibetan Buddhist traditions in this training. For example, in Central Tibet there was Kunpang Tukje Tsondru's Jonang Monastery, Changsem Gyalwa Yeshe's Dechen Monastery, Kunkhyen Dolpopa's Phukmo Cave Monastery and Ngam Ring Monas-

---

62 Tibetan title: *rgya gar gyi chos 'byung*.

tery, Chodrak Pal's Chuzang Monastery, Sazang Mati Panchen's Ganden Monastery, Kunkhyen Nyabon's Tsechen Chode Monastery, Lhagang Monastery, and Tsanchen Monastery, Jetsun Taranatha's Tagten Choling Ngedon Monastery, and more than thirty other monasteries in addition to these. Chalung Thinley Namgyal also instituted the Jonang scholastic curriculum into great Geluk monasteries including Ganden and Drepung. Nevertheless, the nature of our world is that whenever there is progress, there is inevitably decline.

During the Fifth Dalai Lama, both the Jonang and Kagyu traditions were severely suppressed. The reason for this suppression was not because of the superiority or inferiority of their views and practices, or because their educational systems were insufficient, it was due entirely to politics. After this period of decline had waned, the unbroken lineages of these philosophical and contemplative traditions were revived. This is why these traditions have continued to develop unimpaired up until today. Fortunately, the Jonang master Panchen Chogyal's disciple Ratnashri traveled to the Amdo region of Far Eastern Tibet where he began to disseminate *zhentong* philosophical thought. Then, in the year 1365, Rinchen Pal (1350-1435) established Choje Monastery in Dzamthang, and since then, the Jonang tradition has flourished in Amdo.

The Jonang Tradition Today

Today, the sequential lineage of Jonang thought and practice is upheld and preserved by the Jonang monasteries in Kham and Amdo, most particularly those in Dzamthang, and the surrounding regions. Together, these monasteries serve several hundreds of thousands of lay and ordained practitioners. In the monasteries of Dzamthang for instance, there are more than five thousand monks studying *zhentong* Madhyamaka as well as the five major subjects of Buddhist philosophy by authors such as Kunkhyen Dolpopa, his close disciples, and other major masters of the Jonang lineage. In particular, the curriculums of these monasteries emphasize the study and practice of the uninterrupted lineage of the generation and perfection phases of the *Kalachakra Tantra*.

There are also several Jonang monasteries in the Lhatse district of Central Tibet, and more than fifty Jonang monasteries spread throughout the counties of Amdo in Far Eastern Tibet including Ngawa County, Chuchen County, Barkam County, Trochu County, Gade County, Padma County, Chikdril County, and Darlag County. In the Kham region of Eastern Tibet, there are several counties such as Lithang County and Dabpa County where there are Jonang monasteries such as Mingyur Monastery, Dragnag Monastery, Zhingwa Monastery, Delu Monastery, and Thubpa Monastery. Outside of Tibet, the center for the study and practice of the Jonang tradition is Takten Phuntshog Ling Monastery in Shimla, India. This has become a major monastery for meditation practice on the generation and perfection phases of the *Kalachakra Tantra* upheld by the Jonang.

Because this is such an important place for the Jonang outside of Tibet, I would like to give a brief introduction to why this monastery is so significant. Generally speaking, the Jonang tradition is not very well-known among Westerners and to the world beyond the cultural borders of Tibet. However, the reason for this is not because the Jonang is a minor or insignificant tradition. Although some Tibetan Buddhist lineages have vanished while others have been assimilated, currently five major traditions of Tibetan Buddhism exist. In Tibet, these traditions are classified into two great philosophical systems: those which uphold *zhentong* Madhyamaka and those which uphold *rangtong* Madhyamaka. Of these two divisions, the Jonang upholds the system of *zhentong* Madhyamaka. This is to say, of the five Tibetan Buddhist traditions, the Jonang tradition is the major upholder of one of the two great Tibetan Buddhist philosophical systems. In addition to the Nyingma, Sakya, Kagyu, Jonang, and Geluk Buddhist traditions, there is the Bon tradition. While the four Buddhist traditions besides the Jonang and the Bon tradition are officially registered with the Tibetan Government in Exile, the Jonang tradition is not. The reason for this is that when Tibetans fled Tibet into India, there were no representatives of the Jonang tradition to file the proper documents because the great lamas of the Jonang remained in Tibet. This is the major reason why the Jonang is not known to the Western world.

Nevertheless, in 1998 a few Jonang monks escaped Tibet into India, and seeing the importance of sustaining the Jonang tradition, His Holiness the Dalai Lama privately gifted the Jonang Takten Phuntsog Ling Monastery in Shimla, and appointed the Eleventh Jetsun Dampa Khalka Rinpoche as the head of the Jonang in exile. His Holiness also expressed how it is especially necessary for the Jonang to uphold the practice lineage of the generation and perfection phases of the *Kalachakra Tantra*. Then in the summer of 2002, His Holiness visited Takten Phuntsog Ling Monastery for four days in order to bestow empowerments and give teachings from the Jonang tradition, as well as to hold discussions about the initial and future purposes of the monastery. At that time, His Holiness stressed how important it is to sustain the Jonang tradition as it is the only tradition that upholds complete guidance instructions on the *Kalachakra Tantra's* perfection phase yogas. He also expressed his hope that in the future Takten Phuntsog Ling Monastery becomes a meditation center where practitioners of each of the Tibetan Buddhist traditions can come to train in the perfection phase yogas of the *Kalachakra Tantra*.

In the summer of 2003, Jetsun Dampa Kalkin Rinpoche gave teachings on Taranatha's *Quintessential Elixir of the Progressive Stages on the Path* along with several empowerments from the Jonang tradition.[63] Later, the Seventeenth Karmapa Orgyan Thinley Dorje also visited Takten Phuntsog Ling in Shimla and taught the Thirteenth Karmapa's *Song on Understanding the View of the Profound Teachings of the Definitive Zhentong Madhyamaka*.[64] He also expressed how his Karmapa predecessors and he himself had a particular affinity for the *zhentong* Madhyamaka system, and how his principle teachers have emphasized the *zhentong* view.

The Jonang tradition has a long history with profoundly deep scientific systems of learning, and an extended lineage of realised masters. Unfortunately, the Jonang has not been recognized by the Western world and given equal status as the other Tibetan Buddhist traditions

---

63 Tibetan title: *lam rim bdud rtsi'i nying khu*. These empowerments (*dbang*) were Avalokiteshvara from the Gelongma Palmo lineage (*dge slong ma dpal mo'i lugs kyi thugs rje chen po'i dbang*), and White Tara (*sgrol dkar*).

64 Tibetan title: *nges don gzhan stong dbu ma chen po'i zab chos go nyams lta ba'i glu*.

due to its isolation. Now, as this tradition is being registered with the Tibetan Government in Exile, as exemplars of the tradition are living and traveling outside of Tibet, and as significant works of the Jonang are being translated into English and other Western languages, the Jonang will surely receive greater attention. Fortunately, due to the support of His Holiness the Dalai Lama the teachings of the Jonang have already begun to flourish in the world beyond Tibet.[65]

VIEWS AND PRACTICES OF THE JONANG TRADITION

Emptiness & Buddhanature

Mahayana Buddhist traditions regard everything that can be known or the ultimate abiding nature of phenomenal reality as being what is known as "emptiness." This however is not a nihilistic vacuum or a state of nothingness; it is the assertion that there is no fundamental root to existence.

Our current ordinary coarse experiences, the perceptions of all phenomena within one's own mind, including sights, sounds, smells, tastes, and tactile sensations are reflections of an underlying substratum consciousness on the eyes, ears, nose, tongue, and body within an individual's stream of awareness.[66] This universal base or substratum awareness acts like a mirror

---

65 Jamphal Lodro writes "Jonang Tulku Tashi Gyaltsen Rinpoche has established a few centers in New York, Georgia, and Taiwan. He has also sponsored the Great Jonang Prayer Festival in Bodhgaya, India where over a thousand monks have gathered to celebrate the tradition for five days each year since 2002. There are also a few Dzamthang lamas who have established centers in large cities within China, and now many Chinese have taken an interest in the Jonang practice instructions of the *Kalachakra Tantra*."

66 Substratum consciousness (*kun gzhi rnam shes*) is the eighth in the eightfold delineation of consciousness described within the Yogacara School of Mahayana Buddhism. Substratum consciousness serves as the receptacle and repository for the latent impressions and memory traces (*bag chags*) created by bodily, vocal, and mental activities until they are reactivated. The other seven types of consciousness are: the five sensory consciousnesses (*dbang po'i rnam shes*) including visual consciousness (*mig gi rnam shes*), auditory consciousness (*rna ba'ii rnam shes*), olfactory consciousness (*sna yi rnam shes*), gustatory consciousness (*lce'i rnam shes*), tactile consciousness (*lus kyi rnam shes*), discursive mental consciousness (*yid kyi rnam shes*), emotionally defiled consciousness (*nyon mongs pa'i yid kyi rnam shes*).

which reflects images onto itself. In this way, what seems to be external appears within one's own awareness. Because of this, objective references cannot be even slightly established as intrinsically enduring and real.

Since objects don't actually exist separate from the proliferations of an individual's substratum consciousness, everything perceived by ordinary beings is a deception.[67] By regarding what exists to be untrue, like the apparitions of an illusionist, all things constant and stable in conventional reality are understood to be nonexistent or like illusions. However, the stream of one's own substratum awareness, the ever-abiding empty nature of everything is continuously permanent and everlasting.[68] No matter what happens, this continuum maintains an unchanging great bliss that can never be harmed. Because it is devoid of falsity, it can't deceive. This is why it is said to be truly existent and invariant.

In general, only someone who actualizes sublime Buddhahood is imbued with the omniscient consciousness that instantaneously cognizes non-deceptive phenomena, and everything that can be known which is the true nature of reality. Through their great loving compassion, a Buddha becomes a source of refuge with inconceivable powers and capacities for protecting illimitable deluded beings. Similarly, Buddha Shakyamuni manifests like reflections on a mirror by appearing in infinite forms in order to benefit beings. Names that have been given for this innate potential for enlightenment include: "Buddhanature," "one's basic mode of being," "one's fundamental enlightened essence," or the "Ultimate Three Jewels."

Within all of us, in the mind-stream of every sentient being, from time without beginning up until this very moment, there is an innate enlightened essence that pervades. This essence is likened to a jewel within a vase,

---

67 The latent unconscious inclinations and residual karmic tendencies *(bag chags)* within substratum consciousness are the source of these "proliferations of substratum consciousness." The proliferations *(mched pa)* are the reactivations of the latent traces that are likened to seeds *(sa bon)* that ripen into fruits *('bras bu)* of experience.

68 The basis of pristine awareness *(kun gzhi ye shes)* is a term differentiating the basic underlying nature of pristine wisdom awareness from that of substratum consciousness. It is a technical term used in particular by Dolpopa Sherab Gyaltsen and subsequent Jonang authors.

an infant within a womb, or a treasure beneath the ground.[69] Due to the obscuring forces of passion, aggression, and ignorance, ordinary beings have not recognized this innate essence. Up until now, we have wandered aimlessly throughout endless cycles of samsaric existence without recognizing our own potential. However, through perfect introspection, it is possible to recognize this actual abiding mode of our being.

For those who do not immediately recognize their own nature through contemplative practice, there is the untainted wisdom-mind of the Buddha Shakyamuni, and commentaries by authors such as the protector Regent Maitreya, those by the Six Ornaments which beautify our world, and those by the Two Excellent Ones which offer us guidance along the path of meditation.[70] Alternatively, by relying on the oral instructions of a qualified Jonang master who is endowed with both knowledge and realization, and can directly introduce the enlightened essence through their own assurance, a practitioner will discover how to develop confidence and conviction in their own innate essence. Then, by cultivating meditative stabilization on what is introduced, a practitioner begins to practice the profound path of the Six Yogas, and the completion phase of the *Kalachakra Tantra*. By acquiring the signs and indications of yogic success, an adept will gradually progress along the path of meditation until Buddhahood is born within. Unless we manifest the seed of Buddhahood that lies dormant within ourselves, we will never find a shiny new Buddha elsewhere, as the cause of being a Buddha does not exist anywhere else.

Zhentong: Extrinsic Emptiness

As for the extraordinary philosophical view of the Jonang tradition, it is referred to as "zhentong," "other emptiness" or "extrinsic emptiness." The

---

69   This is a reference to the nine similes of enlightened essence from the *Uttaratantra*, the *Unexcelled Continuum*: "A Buddha in a rotten lotus, bees amidst honey, a kernel in its husk, gold in grime, a treasure underground, shoots from a small fruit, a figure of the Victor in a tattered rag, a universal king in a wretched woman's womb, a precious image in clay. Likewise, ones' inherent nature is obscured by the distortions of fleeting afflictions, enlightened essence dwells within all beings."

70   The "Six Ornaments" are the six great Indian Buddhist philosophers: 1) Nagarjuna; 2) Aryadeva; 3) Asanga; 4) Vasubandhu; 5) Dignaga; 6) Dharmakirti.

reason why it is called "other" or "extrinsic" emptiness is that this view articulates how the ultimate nature of reality is free from or empty of everything "other" than its absolute essential nature. In other words, it is empty of everything that is false in superficial relative reality. Because this is the assertion, this view is referred to as "emptiness of other." Therefore, it is said that those who uphold this *zhentong* view regard conventional reality as *rangtong*, or empty of its own intrinsic existence while they regard ultimate reality as empty of everything other than itself.

In general, there is the tradition within Tibetan Buddhism of certain scholars criticizing and refuting philosophical views and tenets that oppose their own systems of thought. For example, the Sakya scholar Gorampa (1429-1489) criticized Tsongkhapa (1357-1419) on the Sixty Drong Tsong Points, and the scholar Taktsang (born 1405) further burdened him with the Eighteen Great Loads of Contradiction. Similarly, some scholars have turned against the Jonang tradition in their attempts to dispute its views. Perhaps these people have their own particular agenda, or perhaps they have simply misinterpreted the meaning of Jonang views and tenets due to the depth and profundity of these views. Whatever the case may be, this kind of partiality does exist. It could also be that the primary reason why such criticisms persist is that the central view of the Jonang tradition is that the ultimate nature of reality is truly existent, and since it is well-known to Buddhists that "all phenomena lack true existence," the *zhentong* view is unfit for these critic's ears.

Previously in India, there was a philosophical system known as Samkhya, and their philosophy proposed a primary substance from which everything known was created.[71] Critics of the *zhentong* view treat it like they are refuting the Samkhya notion of a truly existent substance, and then they act as if they are refuting the Jonang *zhentong* view. Putting aside all biases and

---

71 The Samkhya (*grangs can pa*) system of classical Indian philosophy was developed by the sage Kapila in the seventh and early eighth centuries B.C.E. The basic tenet of this dualistic philosophical system is that the entire universe is derived from two principles: the primary animate principle (Skt: *purusa*), and the primary inanimate principle (Skt: *prakirti*) interfusing to create three qualities (Skt: *gunas*) which then interact to create the basic intelligence (Skt: *buddhi*) out of which egotistic identity is born.

prejudices, let's suppose that we can prove that the Samkhya philosophy is unequivocally mistaken. Even if we concede this, what Jonang scholars call the "truly existent enlightened essence," or "the ultimate nature of reality," is not the same as the fundamental principle established by the Samkhya system. What Mahayana Buddhists know as the true existence that is to be negated is easily understood to be different from what the *zhentong* view asserts, and what the *zhentong* view asserts is easily understood to be different from what the Samkhya system asserts.

What Mahayana Buddhists refer to as the truly established "ultimate nature of reality" is in fact exceedingly different from the true existence that is to be negated.[72] The reason for this is that the true existence that is to be negated can only be known by the conceptual minds of ordinary beings, the delusional awareness that is spoiled by ignorance. Since the actual meaning of Buddhanature or enlightened essence is discovered through the pristine wisdom of meditative equipoise that is realised by exalted beings, it is an authentic discovery. In fact, their finding it makes it true. If their discovery were inauthentic, then the pristine wisdom of meditative equipoise would have to be conceptual.

If something is not in accord with the actual meaning of what can be discovered, and if it can deceive the conceptual mind, then it can't be accepted as true. Because of this, the pristine wisdom of meditative equipoise realised by exalted beings is found to be true, and is said to be truly existent. This is due to the fact that the ordinary conceptual mind cannot affirm or deny the actual meaning that is discovered by exalted beings. For instance, let's suppose that the ultimate nature of reality was not truly existent. If it lacked true existence, then it could deceive those minds that perceive it. Therefore, no one could prove it to be true. Since this is so, it is logical to assert that the ultimate nature of reality is truly existent because what is truly existent does not deceive those who perceive it. If this was not the case, and perversions

---

72 Jamphal Lodro writes: "Because adherents of the Jonang *zhentong* philosophical view accept that it is necessary to realize the absence of the twofold identity of an inherent ego and phenomena in order to become a Buddha, and because it is a common Buddhist view that these two types of self-fixation cause beings to wander throughout samsara, isn't it a bit strange that people criticize this view?"

were real, then everyone would want to continually assert their own absurdities based upon their deceptions.

Some say that the not finding of anything by the conceptual mind is discovering the ultimate nature of reality. Actually, the meaning of this conceptual not finding is only an indication of the discursive dualistic mind. A mind free from dualistic perceptions will certainly find the actual meaning. If a mind free from dualistic perceptions could not find the actual meaning, then this non-dual mind perceiving the actual nature of reality would not be found to be meaningful either. Nevertheless, trying to maintain a mind that continually relates to its dualistic perceptions is tiresome.

Besides these sadly meager criticisms, the most controversial themes in Jonang philosophy are its views on the ultimate nature of reality, and its explicit negation of emptiness. Although scholars who uphold nothingness such as those who uphold a view of intrinsic emptiness or *rangtong* claim to refute *zhentong* by means of extensive scriptural quotations or through reasoning, these critics have selected small portions of the writings on *zhentong*, and they have not fully elaborated upon them. This is why it is said that those who uphold the view of intrinsic emptiness have failed to recognize the ultimate nature of reality.

The reason for this is that these scholars regard Shakyamuni Buddha's final set of teachings, the Third Turning of the Dharma Wheel to be errant, and only of provisional meaning.[73] Because the Buddha taught three successive Turnings of the Dharma Wheel in order to instruct his disciples more and more thoroughly, it is impossible that the Buddha's final Turning of the Dharma Wheel would be provisional. In addition to this, the Buddha of the future, the victorious Maitreya commented on this final set of teachings as being definitive in meaning. Similarly, Arya Asanga who was prophesized by the Buddha himself as someone who would distinguish the definitive meaning from the provisional meaning of the sutras stated that the ultimate definitive meaning of the Buddha's teachings is found within his final set discourses.

---

73 Provisional meaning (*neyartha, drang don*) as opposed to definitive meaning (*nitartha, nges don*). These are interpretive schemas employed to the Three Turnings of the Dharma Wheel.

Though some say that Nagarjuna did not teach *zhentong*, this is not entirely accurate. Nagarjuna composed a collection of hymns praising the enlightened intent of the Buddha's final Turning of the Dharma Wheel, and these are perfect exclamations of *zhentong*. The fact is that those who uphold *rangtong* or intrinsic emptiness as a fundamental principle of reality do not have specific scriptural sources to prove this. Consequently, they have created internal contradictions that only have led to quarreling. Fortunately, those who uphold *zhentong* or extrinsic emptiness do not have these contradictions since they arrive at the enlightened intent of the Buddha simply by relying on the scriptural sources of Maitreya and Arya Asanga.

Furthermore, though those who uphold a *rangtong* view do not claim that the ultimate nature of reality is truly existent, this is impossible according to the sublime teachings on emptiness. The reason for this is that if the ultimate nature of reality were emptiness, it would become superficial like the relative nature of reality, and it would therefore lack true existence. This is to say that the ultimate nature of reality would not be able to withstand penetrative investigation. Ultimate and relative reality would then collapse into each other.

Six Yogas of the Kalachakra

One may wonder what kind of path leads to the manifestation of the enlightened essence that is indivisible from the essential base and fruition, and which exists within oneself and all beings as Buddhahood appearing in its three awakened dimensions.[74] According to the Jonang tradition, although there are numerous paths towards awakening, the main path is that of actualization through reliance upon the six auxiliary perfection-phase yogas of the *Kalachakra Tantra*. This is the foremost path of expedience according to the Jonang tradition's unique means of meditation.

---

74 The three dimensions or three enlightened bodies of Buddhahood (*trikaya*, *sku gsum*) are: dimension of emanation (Skt: *nirmanakaya*, Tib: *sprul sku*), dimension of rapture (Skt: *sambhogakaya*, Tib: *longs sku*), and dimension of ultimate reality (Skt: *dharmakaya*, Tib: *chos sku*).

In order to perform these yogas, it is necessary to first prepare by practicing the five common preliminaries. Then, once these are completed, one practices the two uncommon preliminaries of the perfection phase until it is time to integrate the Six Yogas of the perfection phase into one's own experience. A brief summary of the five common preliminaries is as follows.

1. Understand how the Three Jewels are genuine; understand how the Buddha was genuinely an awakened being; and understand how through knowing the Buddha's teachings as authentic, an ordinary being can become a Buddha. Through understanding these points to be valid, decide through your own conviction what are the perfect sources of refuges, then make prostrations, and seek refuge with your body, voice, and mind.

2. Contemplate that all sentient beings were once your extremely kind parents, and think how by relying on the awakening mind of bodhicitta that benefits others how you will be established in the enlightened state of Buddhahood. Knowing what is to be attained, decide to train your mind.

3. In order to give rise to the profound perfection phase of the *Kalachakra Tantra* within the continuum of your mind-stream, and in order to purify mental and emotional obscurations, negativities, and obstructions, visualize the sublime form of Vajrasattva, and recite the one hundred-syllable mantra.

4. In order to accumulate meritorious and favorable conditions, make the perfect gesture of generosity through offering mandalas.

5. Because all blessings stream-forth from enlightened masters, practice guru yoga by mingling your mind inseparably with your root teacher.

These are the common preliminaries.

Once the appropriate accumulations of these common preliminaries have been performed, a practitioner progresses onto the uncommon preliminaries which are exclusive to the perfection phase yogas of the

Kalachakra Tantra. According to the secret Vajrayana, in order to reverse involvement in delusory experiences and adversarial circumstances, the generation phase of the co-emergent Kalachakra deity is practiced. After meditation on the generation phase has been cultivated, the initial postures of the *Kalachakra Tantra* perfection phase are performed. Through the support of multiple bodily postures, and specialized means of abiding in tranquility, one accomplishes the ten signs of inner radiance.[75] These are the two uncommon preliminary practices.

Next are the primary practices of the six auxiliary perfection-phase yogas of the *Kalachakra Tantra.* These are as follows.

1. The first yoga is withdrawal. Supported by the practice of yoga throughout the day and night, the adept absorbs, stabilizes, and dissolves the ten vital winds into one's central channel according to the suitable degrees of rescission.[76] Through this yogic process, the six daytime and four nighttime signs appear, and the adept will accomplish inconceivable perceptions of objects as empty forms.

2. The second yoga is meditative concentration. Through this yoga, perceptions of empty forms, and the awareness of an inner perceiver unify indivisibly. The adept then experientially engages in the five empty forms as equal to the five external references of form, sound, smell, taste, and tactile sensations.

3. The third yoga is harnessing one's life-force. By relying upon the yoga of the vital winds, the vigorous method of harnessing one's life sustaining force, and through the yoga of meditative concentration which interfuses awareness and empty forms, the five primary

---

75 The ten signs of inner radiance (*'od gsal rtags bcu*) are: 1) smoke (*du ba*); 2) mirage (*smig rgyu*); 3) clouds (*sprin*); 4) fire-flies (*me khyer*); 5) sunlight (*nyi ma*); 6) moonlight (*zla ba*); 7) blazing of gemstones (*rin po che 'bar ba*); 8) eclipse (*sgra gcan*); 9) starlight (*skar ma*); 10) rays of light (*'od zer*).

76 The ten vital winds (*rlung bcu*) are: 1) breath (*srog 'dzin*); 2) secretion (*thur sel*); 3) speech (*rgyen rgyu*); 4) digestion (*mnyam rgyu*); 5) metabolism (*khyab byed*); 6) subterranean serpents (*klu*) connected with the eyes; 7) tortoise (*ru sbal*) connected with the heart; 8) Brahma (*tshang pa*) connected with the nose; 9) Devadatta (*lha sbyin*) connected with the tongue; 10) Divine King of Wealth (*nor lha rgyal*) connected with the entire body.

winds and the five subsidiary winds are unified.[77] Drawing these winds into one's central channel and the six subtle chakra centers ceases circulation of the right and left channels, and the adept attains mastery over the channels and winds.[78] Once this yogic technique is stabilized, the adept no longer depends on coarse foods for nourishment but is nourished by the winds.

4. The fourth yoga is retention. Due to mobilizing the life-force, the adept is able to retain the bodily essential fluids and thereby unify empty forms, winds, and awareness. Through this yoga, these three interfuse into indestructible seminal spheres. These spheres continue to reside within the six subtle chakra centers. By relying on this yoga of the secret seminal spheres, the adept equally fuses the subtle essences and the seminal spheres of bliss with the four symbolic seals. Through the practice of repeatedly inducing bliss and peace, immutable bliss and peace are sustained.[79]

5. The fifth yoga is recollection. Through this yoga of recollection, the adept gains powerful mastery over the subtle essences retained by the four symbolic seals. More specifically, by being supported by the symbolic seals of infinite empty forms, and by continually drawing forth the pristine wisdom of the four joys, the adept is constantly inseparable from supreme immutable bliss.

6. The sixth yoga is meditative absorption. Mastery over the yoga of recollection, and reliance upon the pristine wisdom of constant, inseparable, supreme immutable bliss, the adept gradually diffuses the

---

77   The five primary vital winds (*rtsa ba'i rlung nga*) are: 1) life-upholding (*srog 'dzin*); 2) upward-moving, (*me mnyam*); 3) pervading (*khyab byed*); 4) fire-equalizing (*gyen rgyu*); 5) downward-clearing (*thur sel*).

78   These six chakras are: 1) space at the top of the head (*gtsug gtor nam mkha'*); 2) bliss at the forehead (*dpral ba bde ba*); 3) delight at the throat (*mgrin pa longs spyod*); 4) actuality at the heart (*snying kha chos*); 5) emanation at the navel (*lte ba sprul pa*); 6) bliss sustaining at the secret place (*gsang gnas bde skyong*). There are three main channels (*rtsa*) in the subtle body: the central channel (*dbu ma*), the right channel (*ro ma*), and the left channel (*rkyang ma*).

79   These four symbolic seals (*phyag rgya bzhi*) are: 1) Great Seal (*phyag rgya chen po*); 2) Actual Seal (*chos kyi phyag rgya*); 3) Sacred Commitment Seal (*dam tshig phyag rgya*); 4) Activity Searl (*las kyi phyag rgya*).

twelve impure seminal spheres. By means of stabilizing meditative absorption, and successively progressing along the twelve stages of absorption, the adept accomplishes minor coalescence with the co-emergent Kalachakra deity's body.

Gradually, the adept unifies emptiness and bliss equally in order to interfuse the male and female consorts in enlightened embrace. This is the Kalachakra deity co-emergently residing within one's conscious continuum. Actualizing the Kalachakra deity's body, voice, and mind within oneself as a continuously experienced stream of bliss allows the adept to manifest in countless ways in order to effortlessly and spontaneously bring happiness to beings. This is the supreme fruition of Buddhahood.

Methods of magical apparition meditation for
Receiving the great bliss of a physical consort as an empty form,
And as the constant and perpetual realization of playfulness,
Continue to multiply countlessly in the snowy mountains!

CHAPTER VIII

THE GELUK TRADITION

HISTORY OF THE GELUK TRADITION

The Yellow Hat

As prophesized by the Buddha in his collection of sutra discourses titled the *King of Conferring Advice*, the King of Dharma Jetsun Tsongkhapa established Ganden Monastery or the Victorious Sanctuary of Joy on a mountainside outside of the city of Lhasa, in Central Tibet.[80] The tradition of this place was initially referred to as "Gandenpa" after the name of the monastery, and was later popularized as "Geluk."

When the tenth century monk, and reviver of the Buddhist ethical codes, Lumey Tsultrim Sherab departed the great master Gongpa Rabsal for a journey into Central Tibet, he was given a yellow hat to wear in remembrance of his teacher. From that time onwards, the monks of the Geluk tradition have worn yellow hats as a representation of their dedication to the Vinaya or the Buddha's ethical teachings. In order to signify his own adherence to the Vinaya, Tsongkhapa also wore a yellow hat while teaching, and eventually the Geluk became known as the "yellow hat" tradition.

---

80 Tibetan title: *gdams ngag 'bogs pa'i rgyal po.*

The Great Jetsun Tsongkhapa

Jetsun Tsongkhapa Lozang Drakpa (1357-1419) was born in Tsong-kha, in the Domey district of Amdo, Far Eastern Tibet. At the age of eight, Tsongkhapa received ordination vows from Choje Dondrup Rinchen, and was given the name "Lozang Drakpa." When he was sixteen years old, he departed his family for Central Tibet where he met many incredible masters including Lama Uma, Choje Remdawa, the accomplished adept Karmavajra from Lodrak, and the Jonang masters Chogle Namgyal and Nyawon Kunga Pal. Tsongkhapa then spent a decade with these great teachers studying the commentaries and practical instructions from each of the different Hinayana, Mahayana, and Vajrayana Buddhist traditions. Eventually, he became unrivalled in his knowledge of the general topics of the Buddhist sciences, and his reputation as a scholar and adept spread in every direction.

Tsongkhapa received full ordination from Khenpo Tsultrim Rinchen who maintained the precept lineage of the great Pandita Shakya Shri, and through his careful observation of even the most minor vows, he became respected as the foremost holder of the Vinaya monastic code in Tibet. With the support and respect of the great scholars and adepts of his time, Tsongkhapa initiated the Great Prayer Festival in Lhasa where during the inauguration he placed jeweled crowns on top of the Jowo Shakyamuni, Manjuvara, and Avalokiteshvara statues in the central temple.

At the age of fifty-three, Tsongkhapa founded Namgyal Monastery in the highlands of Central Tibet where he taught extensively. Among his most renowned compositions are *The Essential Elucidation of the Definitive and Provisional Meanings*, *The Illuminated Lamp of Five Stages*, *The Great Exposition on the Stages of the Path*, and *The Great Exposition on the Stages of Tantra*.[81] Tsongkhapa also had many students including four close disciples, five accomplished disciples, four impoverished disciples, eight pure disciples, two principle disciples, four chief disciples, ten luminaries of

---

81   Tibetan titles: *drang nges legs bshad snying po, rim lnga gsal sgron, lam rim chen mo, sngags rim chen mo.*

the teachings, six bodhisattvas, two distinguished and learned scholars, and six great disciples who spread Buddhism widely throughout Tibet.

After Jetsun Tsongkhapa passed away, his seat at Ganden Monastery was held by his disciple Gyaltsab Dharma Rinchen (1364-1432), and then by Khadrup Gelegs Pal Zangpo (1385-1438). This succession has continued up to the present day, the one hundred-and-first holder of the Ganden throne. Tsongkhapa had many disciples throughout the three provinces of Tibet, and as a consequence the teachings and lineage of Ganden have flourished.

Geluk Monasteries

In the year 1419, Tsongkhapa's disciple Jamyang Choje (1379-1449) established the great monastic complex of Tashi Drepung Monastery, and in that same year, Jamchen Choje founded Sera Thegchen Monastery. Then, in the year 1447, Tsongkhapa's disciple and the First Dalai Lama, Gendun Drub (1319-1474) established Tashi Lunpo Monastery. Together, these three monasteries along with Ganden are the four major monastic complexes of the Geluk tradition in Central Tibet, and have served as the models for other Geluk monasteries.

In particular, within the Amdo region of Far Eastern Tibet, there are four Geluk monasteries known as the "Four Great Monasteries of the North" which follow the study and meditation curriculums upheld by the four major Geluk monasteries in Central Tibet. Prior to the life of Jetsun Tsongkhapa, in the year 1349, Choje Dondrup Rinchen founded Chakyung Tekchen Yontan Dargye Monastery in Domey, and this later became a monastery which upholds the teaching and practice lineages of the Geluk tradition; in 1604, Gyalse Donyod Gyatso established Gon Lung Jampa Monastery; in 1649, Chuzang Namgyal Paljor established the great Chuzang Ganden Mingyur Monastery in Domey; in 1650, Khenpo Tsadpo Dondrup Gyatso established Serkhog Ganden Damcho Monastery. Together, these represent the Geluk tradition's "Four Great Monasteries of the North."

In 1709, Jamyang Shepa (1648-1721) founded Labrang Tashikhyil Monastery in Northeastern Tibet, and smaller subsidiary monasteries have been built all over Tibet. Today, Ganden Monastery, Drepung Monastery, and Sera Monastery have been re-established in India with more than ten thousand monks, and the Geluk tradition continues to develop centers for learning all over the world. The basic model for the educational curriculum of the Geluk tradition that continues to be employed up to today was designed by Tsongkhapa and his two closest disciples, Gyaltsab Darma Rinchen and Khadrup Gelegs Pal Zangpo. In addition to these primary studies, variant curriculums have been developed by later masters of the lineage such as Sera Jetsun Chokyi Gyaltsen (1469-1546), Panchen Sonam Drakpa (1478-1554), Zhang Gaway Lodro, and Jamyang Shepa.

VIEWS AND PRACTICES OF THE GELUK TRADITION

The Three Aspects of the Path

The initial phase for anyone seeking spiritual freedom and omniscient Buddhahood is becoming genuinely disenchanted with every aspect of samsara. This process begins with a practitioner recognizing how extremely rare and precious one's present human life is, and how we are now endowed with eight freedoms and ten fortunes.[82] By contemplating the certainty of death, the uncertainty of the time of death, and how through the power of actions and emotions everything positive and negative is created within the world of samsara, a practitioner feels compelled to act diligently in this life. With a broad vision of reality, and by analyzing again and again through scrip-

---

82   The eight freedoms (*dal ba brgyad*) are: 1) Being free from the life of a denizen in hell; 2) Being free from the life of a hungry-ghost; 3) Being free from the life of an animal; 4) Being free from the life of a god; 5) Being free from the life of a barbarian; 6) Being free from believing in extreme perverted views; 7) Being free from living during a time when there is no teachings of a Buddha; 8) Being free from living a life as a mute idiot without healthy sense-faculties; The ten fortunes (*'byor ba bcu*) are: 1) The fortune of living the life of a human being; 2) The fortune of living in a place where there are teachings of a Buddha; 3) The fortune of living with intact sense-faculties; 4) The fortune of not holding inexplicably perverted views; 5) The fortune of being endowed with faith; 6) The fortune that a Buddha has appeared; 7) The fortune that a Buddha has taught; 8) The fortune that the Buddha's teachings continue to exist; 9) The fortune that it is possible to understand the Buddha's teachings and live accordingly; 10) The fortune that spiritual teachers are accessible.

tures and reasoning, one comes to understand genuine happiness. This wish that is generated to be free and to reverse everything within the three realms of samsara is known as "renunciation," and is the basis of the Buddhist path of transformation.

If a practitioner is able to generate authentic renunciation within his or her stream of awareness, then every virtue and every karmic impression created will serve as a source of liberation. Meditating on loving-kindness and compassion, a practitioner then understands that at one time or another, every sentient being has been one's own kind mother. The sincere wish to establish all beings in the ultimate state of complete Buddhahood, and the unaltered state of mind that gives rise to such courage is called "bodhicitta" or the "mind of awakening." Once someone has given rise to this genuine mind of awakening, then whatever that person does progresses them along the Mahayana path, and propels them towards omniscience, as this is the most important practice along the Buddhist path of transformation.

Nevertheless, if an understanding of the insubstantial nature of reality does not arise within one's stream of awareness, and if a realization of both the insubstantial nature of the self and phenomena does not occur, then upsetting emotions will not be remedied. For this reason, the realization of insubstantiality is essential for the freedom of mind. Accordingly, it is imperative that a practitioner ascertain through reasoning the primacy of supreme relativity. This "view of emptiness" is fundamental for progressing along the Buddhist path of transformation.

Because renunciation, the mind of awakening, and the view of emptiness are the three primary points necessary for perfecting the Buddhist path of spiritual transformation, Jetsun Tsongkhapa named these the "three aspects of the path."

Emptiness & Ethics

The uncommon view of the Geluk tradition recognizes the ultimate nature of reality to be refuted as non-existent. This unqualified recognition of ultimate reality, otherwise known as a "non-affirming negation," is very valuable. For instance, since limitless beings from time without beginning have intensely fixated themselves on the false belief in an independent enduring self, this assertion of a non-affirming negation understands the empty nature of all phenomena, and acts as an antidote to this intense fixation. Because this view reverses the habit of mistaking things to be truly existent, it is extremely effective at counteracting the fixation on a permanent self. In addition to this, the ascertainment of the interdependence of all phenomena counteracts the tendency to fall into the pits of perverted views, and secures practitioners success along the path of meditation more than those who lack this understanding.

The particular characteristics of Geluk practice emphasize the common path of renunciation, and giving rise to the mind of awakening. The view of emptiness is then gradually developed through extensive listening to teachings, studying the scriptural tradition, and eventually meditating on personal guidance instructions. In general, Jetsun Tsongkhapa placed most of his attention on explaining the uncommon approach of realizing emptiness as a non-affirming negation. He emphasized how the uncommon views and practices of the Hinayana, Mahayana, and Vajrayana are in alignment with the reasoning of Prasangika Madhyamaka.

As the Buddha taught, the survival of Buddhism depends upon how honestly monks maintain the monastic ethical code of the Vinaya. Even if just a few tantric yogis contradict these ethics, then the teachings of the Buddha are threatened. This is why the maintenance of the Vinaya is so important. This is why there are precise methods for practicing the Vajrayana tantric teachings, and why there are special rituals designed for the renewal of vows for practitioners who have acted in non-ethical ways.

From within the happy grove of deities, the stainless ethical code

Joy and kindness sings the songs of eloquent explanations!

The Geluk tradition swells forth from the vermillion ocean

Of the Buddha's teachings to the North!

EPILOGUE

The Inter-relationship of the Buddha's Essential Instructions

The Five Traditions of Tibetan Buddhism

Even though there are numerous disagreements regarding when the Buddha passed away, in India, Burma, Thailand, Sri Lanka, Cambodia and other countries that generally follow the system of the Sthavira School or the School of the Elders, this year (2005) makes it two thousand, five hundred and forty-nine years since the Buddha's nirvana. In the year 433 of the Buddhist calendar, nine hundred and seventy-seven years after the Buddha's nirvana, during the seventh century C.E., Buddhism was introduced into Tibet by the Dharma King Songtsen Gampo. By the late eighth and early ninth centuries, the Abbot Shantarakshita, the Master Padmasambhava, and the Dharma King Trisong Deutsen had met, and Buddhism had begun to flourish in Tibet. During this time, one hundred and eight scholars from India and one hundred and eight translators of the Tibetan language gathered together at the great Temple of Samye.

This time is known as the early flourishing of the Buddha's teachings. At this time of early flourishing, there was King Trisong Deutsun and the twenty-five disciples of Padmasambhava, eighty accomplished adepts, one hundred and eight great meditators from Chuwori, thirty accomplished adepts from Sheldrak, twenty-five realised masters from Yangdzong Phuk, and many other awareness-holders and adepts were present.

Beginning in the year 901, a seventy year persecution of Buddhism in Tibet began during which the Buddhist communities were banished, and all of the tantras of the early translation period were stored away in safe places by tantric practitioners, allowing these texts to remain uncorrupted. Then, in 973, there was a revival of Buddhism. Ever since this revival and later flourishing, the translations of the Buddha's teachings that occurred during that time have been designated as those of the new translations.

The Sakya, Kagyu, Jonang, and Kadam all arose during this new translation period. Later, the instructions of the Kadam tradition were assimilated into a more general teaching tradition. More specifically, the oral Kadam tradition was expanded and reinterpreted by Tsongkhapa to become known as the new Kadam or Geluk tradition. In addition to these major traditions, there were also many minor oral instruction lineages such as the Shalupa, Orgyenpa, Wodongpa, and so forth. Although some of the philosophical influences of these traditions have survived, their great enlightened activities never spread. Today in Tibet, the Sakya, Kagyu, Jonang, and Geluk are the four most well known surviving traditions of this early translation period.

Sakya Monastery was established by Kontan Konchok Gyalpo in 1073, making it the oldest of these four traditions. Not long after this time, the forefather of the Kagyu tradition, Lotsawa Marpa Lodro was born. During his lifetime, Marpa traveled to India in order to bring back essential guidance instructions of the Buddha to Tibet. Although this accomplishment helped to increase Buddhism in Tibet, it did not firmly establish the Kagyu tradition. It was not until Marpa entrusted the Buddha's essential instructions to his disciple Milarepa, who then transmitted these instructions to Gampopa that the Kagyu tradition was established. Gampopa founded Gampo Mountain monastic center in the year 1121, commencing the development of the Kagyu tradition as we know it today.

The Jonang tradition was established almost one century after the Kagyu tradition. Even though many of the sutras and tantras that elucidate Buddhanature were translated from Sanskrit into Tibetan during the time of the Abbot Shantarakshita, the Master Padmasambhava, and the Dharma King Trisong Deutsen, a tradition of extensively explaining *zhentong* Madhyamaka did not develop from these early translations. Later, Zi Lotsawa Gaway Dorje initiated the system of sutra *zhentong*, and then Dro Lotsawa Sherab Drakpa initiated the system of tantra *zhentong* in Tibet. The Jonang tradition then firmly took root in the year 1292 when Kunpang Thugje

Tsondru established the monastic seat in Jomonang. From this time onwards, the teachings of the Jonang have sustained. In the fourteenth century, the great master of the Jonang, Kunkhyen Dolpopa Sherab Gyaltsen then unified the sutra and tantra teachings, causing the view and practices of the Great Madhyamaka *zhentong* to spread far and wide, like the tremendous roar of a lion.

In 1407, more than one hundred years after the Jonang tradition had initiated, the great Jetsun Tsongkhapa established Ganden Monastery in the highlands of Central Tibet, commencing the Geluk tradition.

Unity of the Tibetan Buddhist Traditions

Because students have various dispositions and inclinations, there are various teachings to suit the many different types of individuals. With this in mind, it is important to recognize how all of these teachings share the single essential intent of the Buddha, and how all of the learned adepts from both Indian and Tibet transmitted this ultimate intent. In the words of Panchen Lozang Chogyan,

> Co-emergent Yoga, Fivefold Mahamudra, Single Taste, the Four Syllables, Pacification, Severance, Dzogchen, instructions on the view of Madhyamaka and so forth, although these teachings are given various names with seemingly varying intents, if yogis with experience and scholars who understand the definitive meaning of the scriptures and reasoning examine carefully, they will discover that these teachings are of a single intent.

From the words of Panchen Lozang Yeshe who was also the author of a guidance text on Mahamudra,

> Philosophical systems from Utsang to Ngari,
> All of these places share exactly the same teachings of the victor,
> Because of this, refrain from acting like a devil of partiality.
> Instead, increase your radiant jewel-like pure vision.

The Great Fifth Dalai Lama's tutor, Kontan Paljor Lundrup composed a guidance text that covers Mahamudra, Dzogchen, and Madhyamaka; the Geluk scholar Khadrup Je praised the teachings of Dzogchen in his response to the questions of Geshe Sangye Rinchen on the ultimate intent; the Nyingma master Jamyang Mipham Rimpoche established how through scripture and reasoning the intent of the Sakya, Geluk, Kagyu, Nyingma, and Jonang are non-contradictory. These are just a few examples that point to how masters of the past have transmitted this ultimate intent.

As these examples show, the motive for studying and practice is one and the same. For this reason alone it is important to remain unbiased with one's faith and understanding of the underlying truth and purpose shared by all of the Buddha's teachings. For if we put efforts into proving or refuting one teaching exclusively over another, this kind of assertive attitude will ultimately be self-defeating.

Just as we have seen, the great founders of the teaching lineages of Tibetan Buddhism were of one wisdom-mind. This is again exemplified in the following words of Panchen Lozang Chokyi Gyaltsen,

> Powerful siddha Padmasambhava, your manifestation Atisha, and your glorious reincarnation Tsongkhapa, in no one other than you, I go to refuge.

The second Dalai Lama Gedun Gyatso also wrote,

> Awareness-holder and sovereign of all siddhis, Padmasambhava,
> Crown ornament of five hundred scholars, Atisha,
> Almighty Vajradhara who is glorious Tsongkhapa,
> To the dance performance of your myriad manifestations, I bow.

Similarly, Jetsun Tashi Gyatso uttered,

> Boundless brilliance Amitabha, protector Padmasambhava, Atisha and the gentle splendor Tsongkhapa are of one wisdom-awareness whose gestures are like the play of the moon in water. From conviction deep within my heart, I bow hundreds of times over.

Gungtang Rinpoche also wrote in his explicit instructions on the practice of Manjushri,

> Initiator of Buddhism in the Land of Snows, Padmasambhava,
> Composer of the union of the tantras and their meaning, Atisha,
> Composer who dispelled the darkness of confusion, Tsonkhapa,
> You three are inseparable, genuinely established through scripture.

As all the great Buddhist teachers of our times are saying with one voice, "regardless of what tradition you practice, Buddhist practitioners are those who exert themselves through developing devotion, pure vision, purity, prayer, and making offerings." This sentiment is reflected in the condensed biography of Padmasambhava where it reads,

> The prophecy of the Buddha is that in the region of Amdo, Atisha's manifestation will appear as Tsongkhapa. Upon the arrival of this great being in Tibet, joy and happiness will dawn. At that time, the forces of positivity will rejoice.

> At the time of my emanation known as Sakya, there will be a child born into this world from a father named Manjushri, and a mother named Tara whose name will be Sakya Pandita Kunga Gyaltsen, the supreme protector of beings. He will rebuild temples and provide spiritual nourishment for beings. He will expand the secret tantric teachings of the Buddha. He will provide joy and happiness for everyone in Tibet.

An emanation of Manjushri, Nyawon Kunga Pal said,

> Known as Prince Litsavi as the attendant of the Buddha, White Lotus born of the noble family from Kalapa, and the great Nagarjua from Sri Parvata Mountain, the great bodhisattva Dharmodgata from Ponaydan Snow Mountain, Songtsen Gampo from the city of Lhasa, Padmasambhava from the Chamara continent, Shesrab Gyaltsen, at your feet, I supplicate.

Thekwang Chokyi Dorje in his work titled, *Polishing the Ketaka Gem* also wrote,

> The great Jowo, the unequaled precious Gampopa, King of the Dharma Tsongkhapa are all magical manifestations of the great master Padmasambhava. As it is said over and over again, no one has been more kind towards the people and Buddhism of Tibet.

Based on these passages, we can begin to understand how all of these masters are of the same wisdom continuum. Without taking into consideration their mutual level of renunciation and realization, some foolish people continue to hold firmly onto their biased views that one is better and another is worse. Moreover, by asserting or refuting one of these sublime teachings over another, this kind of behavior actually causes divisions among the various traditions, and goes onto instill fear within the minds of practitioners.

The Rimed Spirit

In order to perfect one's practices and become an authentic spiritual person, we can adapt a Rimed or nonbiased approach towards the Buddhist traditions. For instance, Jetsun Tsongkhapa received instructions in Dzogchen practice from the great Nyingma master from Lodrak named Layki Dorje, Madhyamaka instructions from the Sakya master Remdawa Zhonu Lodro, instructions on the Six Yogas of the *Kalachakra Tantra* from Jonang Panchen Chogle Namgyal, and instructions on the *Prajnaparamita Sutras* or *Transcendent Wisdom Scriptures* from Jonang Nyawon Kunga Pal. If Tsongkhapa did not honor these spiritual teachers and the Rimed philosophical spirit, he would not have wanted to receive and practice these various essential instructions.

Like Tsongkhapa, there are numerous masters from the Sakya, Geluk, Kagyu, Nyingma, and Jonang traditions who acknowledge and maintain philosophical understandings from other lineages without contradiction. Another example was the Great Fifth Dalai Lama Ngawang Lozang Gyatso who was a core lineage-holder of the Geluk tradition but also composed an essential guidance text on the Nyingma Dzogchen teachings known as the *Oral Instructions of the Awareness-Holders*. Kunkhyen Longchen Rabjam, a core lineage holder of the Nyingma tradition, received and practiced many profound teachings on the definitive meaning of *zhentong* from the Third Karmapa Rangjung Dorje. Ju Mipham Jamyang Gyatso of the Nyingma tradition asserted a *zhentong* view similar to that of the Jonang in his famous work titled, *The Lion's Roar*. The great Nyingma teacher, Za Patrul Orgyen Jigme completed a three year retreat on the Six Yogas of the *Kalachakra Tantra* from the Jonang tradition and was able to explain this system. Konton Konchog Gyalpo, a lama from the Sakya tradition, was able to give untainted teaching advice from the Nyingma tradition. Jamgon Kongtrul Lodro Thaye, a great exemplar of the Rimed spirit, compiled the *Treasury of Spiritual Advice*, integrating the essential instructions from all eight chariots or practice lineages of Tibetan Buddhism. The Jonang master Kunpang Thugje Tsondru practiced all seventeen lineages of guidance instructions on the *Kalachakra Tantra* in Tibet.

The lineages of Tibetan Buddhism are intertwined through empowerments, transmissions, and guidance instructions to the extent that not even a single one is connected to another. For this reason alone, to regard a tradition with partiality, to look upon one tradition as better than another, is a mistake. Since these traditions are equal doorways to wisdom, they are each beneficial. As the founders and great authors of these traditions have explained, studying and practicing what these traditions have to offer enables us to avoid prejudices. This nonbiased Rimed spirit is especially maintained by His Holiness the Fourteenth Dalai who does an incredible job of upholding the teachings, practices, and explanation lineages of all five Tibetan Buddhist traditions.

The teachings of Tibet's Snowy Land, and every sublime holder of the teachings,

You are one without contradiction, established through genuine transmissions!

Ordinary people make arrogant assumptions due to naive fixations.

Why is there so much babble about attachment and aversion?

CONCLUDING SUPPLICATION

Masters, victorious Buddhas, and the spiritual children of the lineage,
Please consider my descriptions of the elegant enlightened actions of the three times.

May all the exalted wealth of virtue be born within these three times!
May all the corruptions and misdeeds gathered from time without beginning be purified!

Since time without beginning, beings have wandered throughout the ocean of existence,
Searching for a life filled with fame, wealth, and worldly luxuries
Doing nothing but accumulating further karmic debt.

From this time onwards, may the accumulation of all positive merit
Be secured through the activities of my body, voice, and mind!

By attaining the supreme ability through these positive actions,
May I, through means and knowledge accomplish the excellent path,
And teach in order to bring happiness and benefit beings!

May I, in all my lifetimes, have a sublime and excellent spiritual teacher,
And not be separated from the perfect path of awakening!

May I be completely severed from futile and tiresome actions,
And may opportunities for accomplishing great benefit constantly occur!

In particular, may I be thankful to my parents for their kindness in giving me my body,
And may whomever feels even the slightest feelings of weakness or timidity,
May they realize the virtue of bliss and joy of body and mind!

For as long as space pervades,
And for as long as there are sentient beings,
Through the power and intensity of wisdom,
May all beings be beautified, endowed with fortune,
And accomplish the vast happiness that benefits others!

The teachings of the Buddha are pure from the very beginning,
And the upholders of these teachings are connected without deception to the victors!

Through the altruistic intention to perfect the two accumulations,
May all beings be able to spontaneously fulfill all their wishes without hindrance!

BIBLIOGRAPHY

Works Cited

Blos gros grags pa, Mkhan po Ngag dbang. *Jo nang chos 'byung zla ba'i sgron me.* Qinghai: Nationalities Press, 1992.

Byang sems rgyal ba ye shes. *Dpal ldan dus kyi 'khor lo jo nang pa'i lugs kyi bla ma brgyud pa'i rnam thar.* Beijing: Mi rigs dpe skrun khang, 2004.

Lodro, K.R.J. *Bod kyi chos brgyud khag gi chos 'byung dang lta grub mdor bsdus 'khrul sel dad pa'i sgo 'byed ces bya ba bzhugs so.* New Delhi: Indra-prastha Press, 2003.

Further Readings

Dudjom Rinpoche. *The Nyingma School of Tibetan Buddhism.* M. Kapstein and G. Dorje (trans.). vol. I-II. Boston: Wisdom Publications, 1991.

Gyatso, T. (Dalai Lama). *The World of Tibetan Buddhism: An Overview of Its Philosophy and Practice.* Boston: Wisdom Publications, 1995.

Dalai Lama. *Ethics for the New Millennium.* New York: Riverhead Books, 1999.

Gyatso, K.N. *Ornament of Stainless Light: An Exposition of the Kalacakra Tantra.* G.

Kilty (trans.). The Library of Tibetan Classics, 14. Boston: Wisdom, 2004.

Ray, R.A. *Indestructible Truth: The Living Spirituality of Tibetan Buddhism.* Boston: Shambhala Publications, 2000.

Reginald A. Ray. *Secret of the Vajra World: The Tantric Buddhism of Tibet.* Boston: Shambhala Publications, 2001.

Smith, E. G. "Jam mgon Kong sprul and the Nonsectarian Movement," In *Among Tibetan Texts: History and Literature of the Himalayan Plateau.* Boston: Wisdom Publications, 2001.

Stearns, C. *The Buddha from Dolpo: A Study of the Life and Thought of the Tibetan Master Dolpopa Sherab Gyaltsan.* New York: State University of New York Press, 1999.

Thondup, T. *Buddhist Civilization in Tibet.* New York: Routledge and Kagan Paul Inc., 1987.

Williams, P. *Mahayana Buddhism: Its Doctrinal Foundations.* London: Routledge, 1989.

GLOSSARY

A

ABHIDHARMA (*chos mngon pa*): The Buddha's teachings on the inner and outer sciences including philosophy, metaphysics, psychology, phenomenology, and cosmology; the Abhidharma scriptures outline the elements of experience, and the analytical processes for experientially discovering the nature of existing phenomena.

ABHIDHARMA-PITAKA (*mngon chos kyi sde snod*): The collection of Abhidharma scriptures. See "Abhidharma" and "Tripitaka."

ARHAT (*dgra bcom pa*): A spiritual adept who has conquered the inner enemy of disturbing emotions and attained the Hinayana level of enlightenment.

AVALOKITESHVARA (*spyan ras gzigs*): The bodhisattva of compassion; he who gazes upon living beings in every direction in order to alleviate their suffering.

B

BODHICITTA (*byang chub kyi sems*): "mind of awakening" The altruistic wish and practice of benefiting others in order to establish all beings in the ultimate state of enlightened Buddhahood; the actual practice of generating bodhicitta is divided into the bodhicitta of aspiration or the aspiring mind of awakening (*smon pa'i sems bskyed*), and the bodhicitta of application or the applied mind of awakening (*'jug pa'i sems bskyed*).

BODHISATTVA (*byang chub sems dpa'*): A practitioner of the Mahayana who has developed the mind of awakening (*bodhicitta*). There are generally three types of bodhisattvas: 1) those who are like kings, ascending to the throne of buddhahood in order to secure the enlightenment of others; 2) those who are like boatmen, traversing the waters of samsara along with everyone they help; 3) those who are like shepherds, ensuring that their flock is safe before tending to themselves.

BUDDHAHOOD (*sangs rgyas pa*): A completely awakened Buddha; the state in which all defilements are purified, and all enlightened qualities are expanded.

BUDDHA-NATURE (*bde gshegs snying po*): "enlightened essence" The Mahayana concept of a pure permanent luminous essence or nature that pervades all beings, and is the basis for the realization of Buddhahood.

C

CITTAMATRA (*sems tsam pa*): A Mahayana school of Buddhist philosophy that developed in India and was transmitted into Tibet; the Cittamatra school of thought was founded by Asanga in the sixth century C.E., and is a sub-division of Yogachara; its primary philosophical premise is that all appearances are merely the mind and are inseparable from mental perceptions rooted in the universal basis of awareness or the alayavijnana.

D

DHARMA (*chos*): Sanskrit word for the teachings of the Buddha.

DHARMAKAYA (*chos sku*): "ultimate dimension of reality" The ultimate or absolute dimension of everything known and unknown; what is realised and embodied by a Buddha.

DZOGCHEN (*rdzogs pa chen po*): "Great Perfection" The pinnacle of the nine successive vehicles of spiritual attainment in the Nyingma system;

a subtle tantric practice of recognizing the unaltered radiant nature of mind and reality.

E

EARLY TRANSLATION TRADITIONS (*snga 'gyur*): The body of literature and its associated thought and practices translated during the reigns of the Tibetan Kings Trisong Deutsen and Ralpachen in the ninth century; synonymous with "Nyingma" (*rnying ma*) or the "Ancient Tradition."

F

FOUR NOBLE TRUTHS (*'phags pa'i bden pa bzhi*): These four truths are: 1) suffering (*sdug bsngal*); 2) the origin of suffering (*kun 'byung*); the cessation of suffering (*'gog pa*); 4) the path towards the cessation of suffering (*lam*).

G

GENERATION PHASE (*bskyed rim*): The elaborate phase of creative visualization in which an adept generates or develops a meditation deity through sound, imagery, and body gestures. See also "perfection phase."

GREAT MADHYAMAKA (*dbu ma chen po*): "Great Middle Way" Tradition of Mahayana philosophy that developed in India and was transmitted into Tibet; a term used in a wide variety of contexts but is generally synonymous with the zhentong view. See also "Madhyamaka."

GREAT PERFECTION: See "Dzogchen"

H

HINAYANA (*theg pa dman*): "Lesser Vehicle" The Buddhist teachings and approach concentrating on the Four Noble Truths, interdependent origination, and practices of refraining from harmful actions; the vehicle of spiritual transformation concerned with the liberation of the individual from samsara.

I

J

K

KALACHAKRA / KALACHAKRA TANTRA (dus 'khor / dus 'khor rgyud) "Wheel of Time" / "Wheel of Time Continuum" A large tantra of the later translation period, and its related systems of tantric cosmology, medicine, psychology, and meditative sciences.

L

LATER TRANSLATION TRADITIONS (*phyi 'gyur*): The body of literature and its associated thought and practices translated after the eleventh century; these traditions include the Sakya, Kagyu, Jonang, and Geluk; synonymous with "Sarma" (*gsar ma*) or "New Traditions."

M

MADHYAMAKA (*dbu ma pa*): "Middle Way Philosophy" A Mahayana school of Buddhist philosophy that developed in India and was transmitted into Tibet; the Madhyamaka school of thought was founded Nagarjuna in the first century C.E., and is divided into the Prasangika and Svatantrika sub-schools; its primary philosophical view is that of emptiness beyond the extremes of absolutism or nihilism, and does not posit anything as intrinsically existent. See also "Prasangika" and "Svatantrika."

MANDALA (*dkyil 'khor*): A symbolic representation of a central deity in its surrounding environment used as a tantric meditation device for visualization and mental recreation; mandala offerings are used as representations of the entire universe for offering and arranging offerings within tantric rituals.

MAHAYANA (*theg pa chen po*): "Great Vehicle" The Buddhist teachings and approach concentrating on the practices of a bodhisattva through cultivating compassion and the wisdom that realizes emptiness; mahayana schools of philosophy are the Cittamatra and Madhyamaka; the vehicle of spiritual transformation concerned with liberating all beings from samsara.

MAHAMUDRA (*phyag rgya chen po*): "Symbolic Seal" or "Great Seal" A system of instructions and meditation techniques based on the tantric view of transformation according to the Sarma traditions; precise contemplative practices of recognizing the inseparable nature of mind and phenomena.

MAITREYA (*byams pa*): The future Budda. He is the fifth Buddha of this aeon and is currently the regent of Shakyamuni Buddha in the Tushita Pure Land; the author of the Five Treasures of Maitreya transcribed by Asanga.

MANJUSHRI (*'jam dpal*): The bodhisattva of wisdom; he is the embodiment of supreme gentleness and penetrating insight into the empty nature of reality.

N

NAGARJUNA (*klu sgrub*): Indian Buddhist adept who lived during the first century C.E., and the founder of the Madhyamaka school of Buddhist philosophy.

NIRVANA (*mya ngan las 'das pa*): The ultimate extinguishment of the sources of samsara; the state of freedom from the torments of revolving in the endless rounds of birth and suffering; also synonymous with being a Buddha or Buddhahood, the non-dwelling state of unexcelled enlightenment beyond delusions.

O

ORGYAN (*o rgyan*): See "Uddiyana."

P

PANDITA: Indian word for an accomplished scholar.

PERFECTION PHASE (*rdzogs rim*): The subtle phase of tantric practice in which an adept perfects or completes the generation phase, the creative visualization and actualization of his or her meditation deity. See also "generation phase."

POTALA (*po ta la*): Pure Land residence of Avalokiteshvara.

PRASANGIKA (*thal 'gyur pa*): A sub-school of Madhyamaka philosophy developed in India by Buddhapalita and Chandrakirti then disseminated in Tibet; the system of Madhyamaka Buddhist philosophy that refutes an opponents' proposition by identifying and contradicting the consequence of the opponent's thought as extreme.

Q

R

RANGTONG (*rang stong*): "Intrinsic Emptiness" The Madhyamaka philosophical system and view that understands all phenomena to be empty of its own intrinsic nature; opposed to zhentong. See also "zhentong."

RIMED (*ris med*): The syncretic intellectual movement of Tibetan Buddhist traditions during the later part of the nineteenth century that was initiated in Eastern Tibet; refers to the nonsectarian approach to spiritual practices and philosophical understandings of the Tibetan Buddhist traditions.

S

SARMA (*gsar ma*): See "Early Translation Traditions."

SAMSARA (*'khor ba*): The ordinary condition of unenlightened beings that turns endlessly in frustration and suffering; the cycle of existence rooted in not knowing the nature of reality.

113

SAUTRANTIKA (*mdo sde pa*): One of the four major Indian Buddhist philosophical schools; a Hinayana school of Buddhist philosophy that derives its meaning from the sutras, as opposed to the Abhidharma.

SHRAVAKA (*nyan thos pa*): "Hearer" or "Listener" A Buddhist practitioner dedicated to the Hinayana or First Turning of the Buddha's Teachings; understanding the Four Noble Truths, and the lack of an independent self, a shravaka realizes how suffering pervades samsara; the four spiritual stages of a shravaka are: 1) "Stream-Enterer;" 2) "Once-Returner;" 3) "Non-Returner;" 4) "Arhat."

SIDDHA (*grub thob*): An accomplished spiritual adept who has mastered the ability to perform both supreme and ordinray powers or siddhis.

SUTRA (*mdo*): A discourse of the Buddha; a scripture that records the Buddha's Hinayana or Mahayana teachings as opposed to a tantra.

SUTRA-PITAKA (*mdo sde'i sde snod*): The collection of Sutra scriptures. See "Sutra" and "Tripitaka."

SVATANTRIKA (*rang rgyud pa*): A sub-school of Madhyamaka philosophy developed in India then disseminated in Tibet; the system of Madhyamaka Buddhist philosophy that establishes its conclusions based upon autonomous inferences.

T

TANTRA (*rgyud*): A scripture that records the Buddha's Vajrayana teachings as opposed to a sutra.

TATHAGATA (*de bzhin gshegs pa*): An epithet for the Buddha meaning the one who has gone beyond ordinary awareness and therefor transcended samsara.

THREE JEWELS OR THREE PRECIOUS GEMS (*dkon mchog gsum*): These are the sources of refuge for a Buddhist; they are: 1) Buddha; 2) Dharma or Buddha's teachings; 3) Sangha or Buddhist community.

TRIPITIKA (*sde snod gsum*): "Three Collections of Buddhist Scriptures" or "Three Baskets"

These three collections of Shakyamuni Buddha's teachings are the Vinaya-pitaka or collection of ethical codes, the Sutra-pitaka or collection of discourses, and the Abhidharma-pitaka or collection of inner and outer sciences; together, these three collections comprise the Buddhist Canon.

U

UDDIYANA: The country located in the northwest of ancient India where Padmasambhava was born.

V

VAIBHASHIKA (*bye brag smra ba*): One of the four major Indian Buddhist philosophical schools; a Hinayana school of Buddhist philosophy that derives its meaning from the Mahavidhasa Abhidharma.

VAJRAYANA (*rdo rje theg pa*): The Buddhist vehicle of teachings concentrating on taking the fruit of spiritual realization as the path of transformation as opposed to the Hinayana or Mahayana vehicles.

VINAYA (*'dul ba*): The set of the Buddha's teachings that define the Buddhist monastic ethical code.

VINAYA-PITAKA (*'dul ba'i sde*): The collection of Vinaya scriptures. See "Vinaya" and "Tripitaka."

VISHUDDHA (*yang dag*): "Wrathful Vajra Deity" or "Vajra Heruka" "Vishuddha" literally means "perfectly"; it refers to the wrathful deity (Skt: *heruka*) of the vajra family of tantric teachings, and is one of the eight primary practices of the Nyingma.

W

X

Y

YIDAM (*yi dam*): "Meditation Deity" A tantric practitioner's personal deity; one of the three roots or three fundamental practices of the Vajrayana; the practice of performing the generation and perfection phases of visualizing and actualizing a deity.

Z

ABOUT THE AUTHOR AND TRANSLATOR

THE AUTHOR

Shar Khentrul Jamphel Lodrö Rinpoche was born in the Golok region of Amdo, Far Eastern Tibet. As a child, Rinpoche was recognized as a reincarnation or tulku of Getse Khenpo of the Akyung Kongma Sang region of Tibet by several lamas including Khamsang Terton and Drubchen Gyarang Samdrup.

Khentrul Rinpoche is trained primarily in the Jonang Buddhist tradition, and is an adept of the *Kalachakra Tantra* and the distinctive zhentong view. While in Tibet, he studied and practiced at eleven monastic universities, representing each of the five different Tibetan religious traditions. In 1997, Rinpoche was awarded the title "Rimed Master" or teacher of impartial views. In 1999, Rinpoche became a Khenpo at Jonang Dzamthang Tsangchen Monastery under the instruction of Yontan Zangpo Rinpoche in the Amdo region of Tibet. After becoming a Khenpo, Jamphel Lodrö Rinpoche established summer meditation retreats on the *Kalachakra* in several monasteries throughout Amdo.

In the summer of 2000, Shar Khentrul Jamphel Lodrö left his homeland on pilgrimage to the sacred places of the Buddha's life in India. After meeting His Holiness the Dalai Lama in Dharamsala, India, Rinpoche moved to Australia in 2003 where he currently resides.

THE TRANSLATOR

Michael R. Sheehy is a scholar of Tibetan Buddhism who studies contemplative practices. His writing, translation, and research give attention to contemplative and philosophical thought in Tibet, and more broadly, to the relevance of meditation research to the interdisciplinary humanities. Michael's research focuses on the generative, dynamic, and ever-evolving processes of contemplative practices detailed in Vajrayāna yoga and meditation manuals. For over a decade, he worked with monastic communities on-the-ground to digitally preserve rare manuscripts across the Tibetan plateau. Michael studied extensively in Buddhist Asia, including several years studying philosophy and literature in a Buddhist monastery in the nomadic Golok cultural domain of far eastern Tibet. As a visiting scholar at Harvard Divinity School and at the Mind & Life Institute – where he directed programs including Mind & Life Dialogues XXXII in Botswana and XXXIII in India with the Dalai Lama – his focus has been the intercultural dialogue between Buddhism and science. Over the past few years, he has collaborated in interdisciplinary dialogues that interface Buddhism with discourses in the humanities, cultural psychology, and the cognitive sciences.

Michael is a Research Assistant Professor in the Department of Religious Studies and Director of Scholarship at the Contemplative Sciences Center at the University of Virginia. He is a Series Editor for the *Contemplative Sciences* as well as the *Traditions and Transformations in Tibetan Buddhism* book series at the University of Virginia Press. With Klaus-Dieter Mathes (Vienna University), he co-edited, *The Other Emptiness: Rethinking the Zhentong Buddhist Discourse in Tibet*, and his next book will be on the history and philosophy of the Jonang order of Tibetan Buddhism.

RINPOCHE'S VISION

Dzokden was founded with the express purpose of supporting Khentrul Rinpoche in realizing his vision for greater peace and harmony in this world. As our community continues to grow and develop, more and more people are getting involved with this extraordinary effort.

To give you a sense of the scope of Rinpoche's vision, we can speak of eight goals that reflect Rinpoche's short and long term priorities:

IMMEDIATE GOALS

Ultimately speaking, lasting, genuine happiness is only possible through profound personal transformation. Now more than ever, we need methods to develop our wisdom and actualise our greatest potential. It is for this reason that Rinpoche places such a heavy priority on the preservation of the Jonang Kalachakra Lineage. There are four ways in which Rinpoche proposes to do this:

1. **Create opportunities to connect with an authentic and complete Kalachakra lineage in close collaboration with dedicated meditators in remote Tibet.** Our goal is to create all of the supports for practicing Kalachakra in accordance with the authentic lineage masters who have upheld this tradition for thousands of years. We do this by commissioning statues and paintings, writing books and giving teachings around the world. We place particular emphasis on ensuring the authenticity of our materials, drawing on the profound experience of highly realised meditators who are dedicating their lives to these practices.

2. **Establish international retreat centres for the study and practice of Kalachakra.** In order to integrate the teachings into our

minds, it is crucial to have the opportunity to engage in periods of intensive practice. Therefore, we are working to create the necessary infrastructure that will support and nurture the members of our community to engage in both short and long-term retreat. This includes the purchase of land and the construction of everything that is needed to conduct group and solitary retreats. Our long-term aim is to develop a network of such centres around the world, forming a global community that supports a wide variety of practitioners.

3. **Translate and publish the unique and rare texts of Kalachakra masters.** The Kalachakra System has been the subject of countless texts over the course of Tibet's long history. So far, only a small fraction of these texts have been translated and made accessible in the West. While the theoretical texts are important, we aim to focus particularly on the pith instructions that will guide dedicated practitioners to a deeper experience of these profound teachings.

4. **Develop the tools and programs for a structured learning experience.** With pockets of students distributed throughout the world, we believe it is important to make the most of modern technologies to facilitate the process of learning for our students. Our aim is to develop a robust online educational platform that allows our international community to access quality study programs that are intuitive, structured and engaging.

Long-Term Goals

While we each work towards achieving ultimate peace and harmony in our own minds, we must not lose sight of the fact that we exist within the context of a world filled with a great diversity of individuals. These individuals give rise to a wide variety of beliefs and practices that in turn shape how we relate and interact with each other. In this interdependent reality, it is vital to find viable strategies for promoting greater tolerance and respect. To this end, Rinpoche proposes four specific areas of activity:

1. **Promote the development of a Rimé Philosophy through dialogue with other traditions**. With the desire to be constructive members of a pluralistic society, we need to learn ways of reconciling our differences. To this end, we aim to help people develop the positive qualities that promote an attitude of mutual respect, openness to new ideas and an inquisitive desire to overcome our ignorance.

2. **Develop highly realised role models by offering financial support to dedicated practitioners.** In order to ensure the authenticity of our spiritual traditions, it is imperative that there are people who actualise the highest of realisations. Therefore, we aim to create a financial scholarship program which facilitates genuine practitioners who wish to dedicate their lives to spiritual development, regardless of their system of practice. By helping people actualise the teachings, they become positive role models for those around them, inspiring and guiding the generations to come.

3. **Actualise the great potential of female practitioners by developing specialised training programs**. The Tibetan culture has a long history of cultivating highly realised masters through the intensive training of those who are recognised to have great potential. Unfortunately, all too often the search for potential was focused only on male candidates. Rinpoche believes that it is increasingly important to have strong, highly realised, female role models who can help to bring greater balance into our world. For this reason, we are working to develop a unique training program for providing women with the opportunity to actualise their spiritual potential. It is our aim to design a specialised curriculum as well as the financial infrastructure to fully support all aspects of their education.

4. **Promote greater flexibility of mind and a broader understanding of reality through modern educational programs.** In a world that is rapidly evolving, we need to rethink the types of skills that we are teaching our children. The rigid structures of the

past are often ill equipped to prepare students for the challenges that they will face during their lives. Therefore, we aim to develop a variety of educational programs that can help children to become more flexible and more capable of adapting to their context. An important part of these programs is the development of greater awareness of the role that our mind plays in our day-to-day experiences. We also aim to bring reforms into the monastic education system that would help make them more relevant for this modern world.

How can you offer your support?

The above will not be possible without your support and participation. A vision of this magnitude requires a great deal of merit and generosity from many benefactors over many years. If you would like to offer your support, please do not hesitate to contact us.

Dzokden
3436 Divisadero Street
San Francisco, California 94123
United States of America
www.dzokden.org

www.ingramcontent.com/pod-product-compliance
Lightning Source LLC
Chambersburg PA
CBHW081336120626

46546CB00011B/3370

* 9 7 8 1 9 5 8 2 2 9 0 4 0 *